For all of us
May we not be separated

turning to one another

simple conversations to restore hope to the future

margaret j. wheatley

BK

BERRETT-KOEHLER PUBLISHERS, INC.
San Francisco

Berrett-Koehler Publishers, Inc.
235 Montgomery Street, Suite 650
San Francisco, CA 94104-2916
Tel: (415) 288-0260 Fax: (415) 362-2512
www.bkconnection.com

Ordering Information
Quantity sales. Special discounts are available on quantity purchases by corporations, associations,
and others. For details, contact the "Special Sales Department" at the Berrett-Koehler address above.
Individual sales. Berrett-Koehler publications are available through most bookstores. They can also be
ordered direct from Berrett-Koehler: Tel: (800) 929-2929; Fax: (802) 864-7626; www.bkconnection.com
Orders for college textbook/course adoption use.
Please contact Berrett-Koehler: Tel: (800) 929-2929; Fax: (802) 864-7626.
Orders by U.S. trade bookstores and wholesalers. Please contact Publishers Group West,
1700 Fourth Street, Berkeley, CA 94710. Tel: (510) 528-1444; Fax (510) 528-3444.

Printed in the United States of America
Printed on acid-free and recycled paper that is composed of 80% recovered fiber, including 30% post
consumer waste.

Library of Congress Cataloging-in-Publication Data

Wheatley, Margaret J.
        Turning to one another: Simple conversations to retore hope to the future /
        Margaret J. Wheatley.
        p. cm.
        Includes bibliographical references
        ISBN 1-57675-145-7
        1. Life. 2. Communication in small groups. 3. Group decision-making—Religious aspects.
        4. Social action. 5. Cooperativeness. I. Title.

BD435 .W465 2001
177'.2--dc21   .   2001037981

First Edition
06 05 04 03 02 01   10 9 8 7 6 5 4 3 2 1

Book design by A/3, Adrian Pulfer and Ryan Mansfield
Book cover illustration by Vivienne Flesher

You must give birth to your images.
They are the future waiting to be born.
Fear not the strangeness you feel.
The future must enter you
                    long before it happens.
Just wait for the birth,
for the hour of new clarity.

Rainer Maria Rilke

contents

part one

turning to one another

Welcome

I believe we can change the world if we start listening to one another again. Simple, honest, human conversation. Not mediation, negotiation, problem-solving, debate, or public meetings. Simple, truthful conversation where we each have a chance to speak, we each feel heard, and we each listen well.

What would it feel like to be listening to each other again about what disturbs and troubles us? About what gives us energy and hope? About our yearnings, our fears, our prayers, our children?

I wonder if you believe, as I do, that this world needs changing. This book is an invitation to notice what's going on, to clarify your thoughts and experience, and to begin speaking with those around you. What do you see? What are you experiencing in your life and the lives of those you care about? What do you wish were different?

Human conversation is the most ancient and easiest way to cultivate the conditions for change—personal change, community and organizational change, planetary change. If we can sit together and talk about what's important to us, we begin to come alive. We share what we see, what we feel, and we listen to what others see and feel.

For as long as we've been around as humans, as wandering bands of nomads or cave dwellers, we have sat together and shared experiences. We've painted images on rock walls, recounted dreams and visions, told stories of the day, and generally felt comforted to be in the world together. When the world became fearsome, we came together. When the world called us to explore its edges, we journeyed together. Whatever we did, we did it together.

We have never wanted to be alone. But today, we are alone. We are more fragmented and isolated from one another than ever before. Archbishop Desmond Tutu describes it as "a radical brokenness in all of existence." We move at frantic speed, spinning out into greater isolation. We seek consolation in everything except each other. The entire world seems hypnotized in the wrong direction—encouraging us to love things rather than people, to embrace everything new without noticing what's lost or wrong, to choose fear instead of peace. We promise ourselves everything except each other. We've forgotten the source of true contentment and well-being.

But we haven't really forgotten. As the world becomes more complex and fearful, we know we need each other to find our way through the darkness. The yearning for community is worldwide. What can we do to turn to one another?

The simplest way to begin finding each other again is to start talking about what we care about. If we could stop ignoring each other, stop engaging in fear-filled gossip, what might we discover?

Conversation, however, takes time. We need time to sit together, to listen, to worry and dream together. As this age of turmoil tears us apart, we need to reclaim time to be together. Otherwise, we cannot stop the fragmentation.

And we need to be able to talk with those we have named "enemy." Fear of each other also keeps us apart. Most of us have lists of people we fear. We can't imagine talking with them, and if we did, we know it would only create more anger. We can't imagine what we would learn from them, or what might become possible if we spoke to those we most fear.

I hope we can reclaim conversation as our route back to each other, and as the path forward to a hopeful future. It only requires imagination and courage and faith. These are qualities possessed by everyone. Now is the time to exercise them to their fullest.

Meg Wheatley

why I wrote this book

I write a great deal. But this book is very different from anything I've written in the past several years. I'd like to tell a few aspects of my own story to explain why I felt compelled to write this particular book at this time.

For many years, I've been privileged to meet and work with people in many different communities, organizations, and nations. I have been invited into these different places because of my work on leadership and life in organizations. I've been trying to understand how life organizes, and to apply those learnings to how we structure and design human organizations. Nature organizes much more effectively than we humans do, and quite differently. For example, life works cooperatively, not competitively, in networks of relationships where each depends on the other. (Please see my earlier books for more details.)

I have found life to be the best teacher for the dilemmas of these times. How do we live and work in a world that is increasingly chaotic? How do we live and work as an interdependent community and planet? How do we evoke people's innate creativity and caring? What are the values we must preserve as everything changes around us? How can we be together in ways that affirm rather than destroy life?

Most of the people I meet are caring, intelligent, and well-intentioned. They hope that their work will be of benefit to others, that it makes a small difference. I have sat and thought about life-affirming leadership with eleven-year-old Girl Scouts, and with the head of the United States Army, with tribal peoples and with corporate peoples, with religious ministers and with government ministers.

Working in the world, I've grown increasingly distressed. Especially in the last few years, things clearly are not going right. Good people are finding it increasingly difficult to do what they know is best. Whether we're in a small village or a major global corporation, in any country and in any type of work, we are being asked to work faster, more competitively, more selfishly—and to focus only on the short-term. These values cannot lead to anything healthy and sustainable, and they are alarmingly destructive. Even though life is our best teacher, we're not learning her lessons. I believe we must learn quickly now how to work and live together in ways that bring us back to life.

I've explored this distress with tens of thousands of people, and have discovered something obvious and extremely hopeful. We are all human. The unique expressions of culture and tradition that give us such interestingly different appearances are based on the same human desires for learning, freedom, meaning, and love. You and I are yearning for the same things—wherever we are, using whatever means we have available.

It is an increasingly dark time. It is difficult to do good and lasting work. It is seemingly impossible to create healthy change. But people still are basically good and caring. We may feel distressed, overwhelmed, numbed, and afraid. But beneath these feelings, we still desire learning, freedom, meaning, and love.

Because this is a time when we are bombarded with images of human badness, I have been intentionally exploring human goodness. I have learned a great deal from Paulo Freire's work with the very poor of Brazil, and you will read some of those learnings in these pages. The stories and work of others who have taught me are here also—poets, spiritual teachers, everyday people living lives quite different from mine. From them I've learned that no matter how beaten down we are—by poverty, by oppressive leadership, by tragedy—the human spirit is nearly impossible to destroy. We humans keep wanting to learn, to improve things, and to care about each other.

What's truly hopeful is that we already have the means to evoke more goodness from one another. I have witnessed the astonishing power of good listening and the healing available when someone gives voice to their experience. I saw this first in South Africa after apartheid ended. A few of those stories are in these pages. And other stories from those living in very difficult conditions. We may have forgotten how to listen, or how to tell our own story, but these are the skills that will help us now.

I also have learned that when we begin listening to each other, and when we talk about things that matter to us, the world begins to change. A close friend and colleague of many years, Juanita Brown, has shared her experiences in community organizing and corporate strategy, and her belief in everyone's capacity to figure out how to make a difference. Juanita taught me that all change, even very large and powerful change, begins when a few people start talking with one another about something they care about. Simple conversations held at kitchen tables, or seated on the ground, or leaning against doorways are powerful means to start influencing and changing our world.

Beginning in 1998, another friend and colleague, Christina Baldwin, taught me that human beings have always sat in circles and councils to do their best thinking, and to develop strong and trusting relationships. I have now experienced many circles, in many different settings. Whether I'm with a group of friends or strangers, seated in a windowless corporate room or on logs in the African bush, I have learned that the very simple process of council takes us to a place of deep connection with each other. And, as we slow down the conversation to a pace that encourages thinking, we become wise and courageous actors in our world.

Each of these learnings and observations has led to this book. My feelings for this book are best described in Paulo Freire's voice, in words he used in his first book:

From these pages, I hope at least the following will endure: my trust in the people, and my faith in men and women, and in the creation of a world in which it will be easier to love.

how to use this book

The intent of this book is to encourage and support you in beginning conversations about things that are important to you and those near you. It has no other purpose. The book has three sections. Part One contains short essays about things relevant to conversation. I describe the power of conversation to bring us together, how it revives our hope and commitment to work for the changes we want to see in our world. I also describe several conditions that help with good conversation, including simplicity, courage, listening, and diversity. This entire section is meant to encourage you to be the convener and host of conversations. I hope you feel supported to step forward into action, to call together a few friends and colleagues, and start talking about what you most care about.

Part Two contains a few pages of quotes and images. This is the place for you to pause and reflect on what you've read. And to prepare for the work ahead, which is starting conversations. I hope this section inspires you and gives you energy, because the work is now yours to do.

Part Three has ten short "Conversation Starters." These brief essays provide content for your conversations. (You can, of course, just begin your conversations with the issues and dreams that concern you most.) Each of these conversation starters begins with a question. Each contains a story or two, some facts and quotes, and my own comments and interpretations about the topic. I've included some poems as well.

You'll have to be the judge as to which, if any of these materials, are useful to you to start a conversation. You might want to just use the question, or one quote. I tried to keep the essays short so that they could be read aloud in a group, if that seems useful. My greatest hope is that you, as conversation host, will be provoked by these conversation starters, and then decide what works best for you and your colleagues.

Why did I choose these particular ten questions or topics? These are not the only things we need to be talking about. I know there are other issues more relevant to your community or organization. I chose these ten because, in my experience, they lead people into conversations about their deepest beliefs, fears, and hopes. They also help us understand our experience more fully. Because the questions draw out our individual experience and insight, they also reveal our fundamental human goodness. As we speak to each other from this place, we move closer and develop strong relationships. I hope you will try out these questions and see if they work in this way for you, your friends, and your associates.

I do know that even one of these conversation starters can easily lead you into dozens of other meaningful and important topics. Wherever conversation leads you, I trust you will experience how listening and talking to one another heals our divisions and makes us brave again. We rediscover one another and our great human capacities. Together, we become capable of creating a future where all people can experience the blessing of a well-lived human life.

We can change the world if we start listening to one another again. Please join in.

For the Children
Gary Snyder

The rising hills, the slopes,
of statistics
lie before us.
the steep climb
of everything, going up,
up, as we all
go down.

In the next century
or the one beyond that,
they say,
are valleys, pastures,
we can meet there in peace
if we make it.

To climb these coming crests
one word to you, to
you and your children:

        stay together
        learn the flowers
        go light

can we restore hope to the future?

I don't meet many people who are optimistic anymore. It doesn't matter where I am, in what country or organization, or with whom I'm speaking. Almost everyone is experiencing life as more stressful, more disconnected, and less meaningful than just a few years ago. It's not only that there's more change, or that change is now continuous. It's the nature of the change that is upsetting. For example:

A small political incident sets off violence that doesn't end.

A small computer malfunction disrupts lives for days or weeks.

Economic problems in one country cause hardship in many countries.

The undetected rage of a person or group suddenly threatens us or someone we love.

A disease in one location spreads like wildfire into global contagion.

The plagues we hoped to end—poverty, hunger, illiteracy, violence, disease—are growing worse.

These crises appear suddenly in a life or community. They always feel surprising, out of control, and irrational. The world doesn't make sense anymore, and there are no safe places. As sociologist John Berger describes it:

There is no continuity between actions, there are no pauses, no paths, no pattern, no past and no future. There is only the clamor of the... fragmentary present. Everywhere there are surprises and sensations, yet nowhere is there any outcome. Nothing flows through; everything interrupts.

As I listen to many people, in many countries, I'm convinced we are disturbed by similar things. I've listened carefully to many comments, and included some of them here. Taken as a whole, they paint a picture of people everywhere troubled by these times, questioning what the future holds. Here are some of the comments and feelings I've heard expressed:

Problems keep getting bigger; they're never solved. We solve one, and it only creates more.

I never learn why something happened. Maybe nobody knows; maybe it's a conspiracy to keep us from knowing.

There's more violence now, and it's affecting people I love.

Who can I believe? Who will tell me what's really going on?

Things are out of control and only getting worse.

I have no time for my family anymore. I'm living a life I don't like.

I worry about my children. What will the world be like for them?

Confronted with so much uncertainty and irrationality, how can we feel hopeful about the future? And this degree of uncertainty is affecting us personally. It's changing how we act and feel. I notice this in myself and others. We're more cynical, impatient, fearful, angry, defensive, anxious; more likely to hurt those we love.

Certainly, this is not what any of us wants. How can we become people we respect, people who are generous, loving, curious, open, energetic? How can we ensure that at the end of our lives, we'll feel that we have done meaningful work, created something that endured, helped other people, raised healthy children?

What can we do now to restore hope to the future?

what I believe at this time

I've found that I can only change how I act if I stay aware of my beliefs and assumptions. Thoughts always reveal themselves in behavior. As humans, we often contradict ourselves—we say one thing and do another. We state who we are, but then act contrary to that. We say we're open-minded, but then judge someone for their appearance. We say we're a team, but then gossip about a colleague. If we want to change our behavior, we need to notice our actions, and see if we can uncover the belief that led to that response. What caused me to behave that way and not some other way?

Over the years, I've noticed that many of us harbor negative beliefs about each other. Or we believe that there's nothing we can do to make a difference. Or that things are so crazy that we have to look out only for ourselves. With these beliefs, we cannot turn to one another. We won't engage together for the work that needs to be done.

I've been trying to stay aware of my own beliefs for many years. I'm describing some of them here for a few reasons. First, I want to be held accountable for these. I want my beliefs to be visible in my actions. Second, in stating them, you can learn a bit more about me. These are mine—I expect yours may be quite different. And finally, I hope that in expressing mine, you'll be interested in noticing and stating your own.

Here are some of my beliefs that motivate my actions these days.

People are the solution to the problems that confront us. Technology is not the solution, although it can help. We are the solution—we as generous, open-hearted people who want to use our creativity and caring on behalf of other human beings and all life.

Relationships are all there is. Everything in the universe only exists because it is in relationship to everything else. Nothing exists in isolation. We have to stop pretending we are individuals who can go it alone.

We humans want to be together. We only isolate ourselves when we're hurt by others, but alone is not our natural state. Today, we live in an unnatural state—separating ourselves rather than being together.

We become hopeful when somebody tells the truth. I don't know why this is, but I experience it often.

Truly connecting with another human being gives us joy. The circumstances that create this connection don't matter. Even those who work side by side in the worst natural disaster or crisis recall that experience as memorable. They are surprised to feel joy in the midst of tragedy, but they always do.

We have to slow down. Nothing will change for the better until we do. We need time to think, to learn, to get to know each other. We are losing these great human capacities in the speed-up of modern life, and it is killing us.

The cure for despair is not hope. It's discovering what we want to do about something we care about.

simple processes

I would not give a fig for the simplicity this side of complexity,
but I would give my life for the simplicity on the other side of complexity.
Oliver Wendell Holmes

Many of us would like to simplify our lives, and life in general.
Yet I notice how difficult it is to accept and believe in simple solutions
and processes. Everything has become quite complicated. Things that
were simple, like neighborly conversation, have become a technique,
like intergenerational, cross-cultural dialogue.

Once a simple process becomes a technique, it can only grow more
complex and difficult. It never becomes simpler. It becomes the
specialized knowledge of a few experts, and everyone else becomes
dependent on them. We forget that we ever knew how to do things
like conversation, planning, or thinking. Instead, we become meek
students of difficult methods.

In the presence of so many specialized techniques for doing simple
things, we've become suspicious of anything that looks easy. And
those of us who have technical expertise are especially suspicious. I've
seen myself pull back from simple more than once because I realized I
wouldn't be needed any longer. Those are useful moments that force
me to clarify what's more important—my expert status or making sure
the work gets done well. (I haven't always chosen the nobler path.)

There may be another reason why people in general hesitate to believe in simple solutions. If it's so simple, why haven't we thought of it earlier? Why have we invested so much time and money in learning a complicated method? Was all that learning and struggle a waste of time? It's always hard to acknowledge that we've wasted our time. We stay invested in what's complicated just because it took so much time to learn it.

But simplicity has a powerful ally—common sense. If we reflect on our experience, we notice that good solutions are always simple. Much simpler than we thought they'd be. Everyone has this experience, many times over.

Scientists are taught to seek the simpler solution. If there's a choice between two possibilities, they choose the simpler one. Simple solutions are called "elegant" in science. The beauty of the universe expresses itself in simplicity.

This being true, people often laugh when they finally realize there's a simple, commonsense solution. I think it's a laugh of relief, and of recognition—we remember all those other times we were surprised by simple. But I also think we need to give ourselves credit for our struggles with complexity. We can laugh in our realization only because we're on the other side of complexity.

The simplicity of human conversation
**To advocate human conversation as the means to restore hope to
the future is as simple as I can get. But I've seen that there is no more
powerful way to initiate significant change than to convene a
conversation. When a community of people discovers that they share
a concern, change begins. There is no power equal to a community
discovering what it cares about.**

**It's easy to observe this in our own lives, and also in recent history.
Solidarity in Poland began with conversation—less than a dozen workers
in a Gdansk shipyard speaking to each other about their despair,
their need for change, their need for freedom. In less than a month,
Solidarity grew to 9.5 million workers. There was no e-mail then,
just people talking to each other about their own needs, and finding
their needs shared by millions of fellow citizens. At the end of that
month, all 9.5 million of them acted as one voice for change.
They shut down the country.**

**Whenever I read about a new humanitarian relief effort—some of
which have earned the Nobel Peace Prize—it is always a story of the
power of conversation. Somewhere in the description of how it all
began is the phrase: "Some friends and I started talking..."**

**It is always like this. Real change begins with the simple act of people
talking about what they care about. Did they notice a dangerous street
crossing near their child's school? Cancer increasing in a neighborhood?
Landmines maiming their children? Deaths caused by drunk drivers?
It only takes two or three friends to notice that they're concerned
about the same thing—and then the world begins to change. Their
first conversation spreads. Friends talk to friends. Because friends care
about each other, they pay attention to what is being said. Then they
talk to others, and it grows and grows.**

A Canadian woman told me this story. She was returning to Vietnam to pick up her second child, adopted from the same orphanage as her first child. She had seen conditions there on her first visit two years earlier, and had vowed this time to take medical supplies. "They needed Tylenol, not T-shirts or trinkets." She was expressing this to a friend one day, and the friend suggested that the most useful medical thing she might take would be an incubator. She was surprised by the suggestion (she'd been thinking bandages and pills), but she started making phone calls, looking for an incubator. Many calls and weeks later, she had been offered enough pediatric medical supplies to fill four forty-foot shipping containers! And twelve incubators. From a casual conversation between two friends, she and many others self-organized into a medical relief program that made a significant difference in the lives of Vietnamese children. And it all began when "some friends and I started talking."

Stories like this are plentiful. I can't think of anything that's given me more hope recently than to observe how simple conversations that originate deep in our caring give birth to powerful actions that change lives and restore hope to the future.

the courage of conversation

It's not easy to begin talking to one another again. We stay silent and apart for many reasons. Some of us never have been invited to share our ideas and opinions. From early school days and now as adults, we've been instructed to be quiet so others can tell us what to think. Others of us are accustomed to meetings to discuss ideas, but then these sessions degenerate into people shouting, or stomping out angrily, or taking over control of the agenda. These experiences have left us feeling hesitant to speak, and frightened of each other.

But good conversation is very different from those bad meetings. It is a much older and more reliable way for humans to think together. Before there were meetings, planning processes, or any other techniques, there was conversation—people sitting around interested in each other, talking together. When we think about beginning a conversation, we can take courage from the fact that this is a process we all know how to do. We are reawakening an ancient practice, a way of being together that all humans remember. A colleague in Denmark stated it perfectly: "It remembers me what it is to be human."

We can also take courage from the fact that many people are longing to be in conversation again. We are hungry for a chance to talk. People want to tell their story, and are willing to listen to yours. People want to talk about their concerns and struggles. Too many of us feel isolated, strange, or invisible. Conversation helps end that.

A colleague told me that at one professional conference, she gave participants enough time during her session to have real conversations. At the end, people stood up and cheered and applauded.

I find it takes just one person to have the courage to begin a conversation. It only takes one because everyone else is eager for the chance to talk. They're just waiting for someone else to begin it. They aren't quite as brave as you.

Where can we find the courage to start a good conversation? The answer is found in the word itself. *Courage* comes from the Old French word for heart (*cuer*). We develop courage for those things that speak to our heart. Our courage grows for things that affect us deeply, things that open our hearts. Once our heart is engaged, it is easy to be brave.

We only need enough courage to invite friends into a conversation. Large and successful change efforts start with conversations among friends, not with those in power. "Some friends and I started talking…" Change doesn't happen from a leader announcing the plan. Change begins from deep inside a system, when a few people notice something they will no longer tolerate, or respond to a dream of what's possible. We just have to find a few others who care about the same thing. Together we will figure out what our first step is, then the next, then the next. Gradually, we become large and powerful. We don't have to start with power, only with passion.

Even among friends, starting a conversation can take courage. But conversation also gives us courage. Thinking together, deciding what actions to take, more of us become bold. And we become wiser about where to use our courage. As we learn from each other's experiences and interpretations, we see the issue in richer detail. We understand more of the dynamics that have created it. With this clarity, we know what actions to take and where we might have the most influence. We also know when not to act, when right timing means doing nothing.

If conversation is the natural way that humans think together, what gets lost when we stop talking to each other? Paulo Freire, a Brazilian and world educator who used education to support poor people in transforming their lives, said that we "cannot be truly human apart from communication... to impede communication is to reduce people to the status of things."

When we humans don't talk to one another, we stop acting intelligently. We give up the capacity to think about what's going on. We don't act to change anything. We become passive and allow others to tell us what to do. We forfeit our freedom. We become objects, not people. When we don't talk to each other, we give up our humanity.

Freire had a deep faith in every person's ability to be a clear thinker, and a courageous actor. Not all of us feel that kind of faith in each other. But it is a necessary faith if we are to invite colleagues into conversation. We have to believe they have something to offer, and that they're interested in meaningful conversation. Otherwise, there's no sense talking to them. Sometimes, it takes faith to believe that others have as much concern and skill as we do. But in my experience, when the issue is important to others, they do not disappoint us. If you start a conversation, others will surprise you with their talent and generosity, with how their courage grows.

I think the greatest source of courage is to realize that if we don't act, nothing will change for the better. Reality doesn't change itself. It needs us to act. Near where I live, I watched a small group of mothers cautiously meet together to change one thing in their community. They wanted their children to be able to walk to school safely. They were shocked when the city council granted their request for a traffic light. Encouraged by this victory, they started another project, and then another. Each effort built on their success and was more ambitious than the last. After a few years of working to improve their neighborhood, they participated in securing a very large grant from the U.S. government for neighborhood development (tens of millions of dollars). Today, one of those first mothers has become an expert on city housing, won a seat on the city council, and just completed a term as chair of the council. When she tells her story, it begins like all the others: "Some friends and I started talking."

It takes courage to start a conversation. But if we don't start talking to one another, nothing will change. Conversation is the way we discover how to transform our world, together.

the practice of conversation

There are many different ways to host meaningful conversation. Although I've been hosting dialogues since 1993, my trust in and love for conversations is more recent, a direct outcome of what I've learned from the work of two colleagues and friends, Christina Baldwin and Juanita Brown. Each of them, with several colleagues, has pioneered different and extraordinary ways to host conversations that generate deep insights and actions, and a strong sense of community. At the end of this book, I give more detailed information about their work. They are the expert teachers for how to host conversations. I hope you will go directly to them.

I first fell in love with the practice of conversation when I experienced for myself the sense of unity, of communion, that is available in this process. Most of what we do in communities and organizations focuses us on our individual needs. We attend a conference or meeting for our own purposes, for "what I can get out of this." Conversation is different. Although we each benefit individually from good conversation, we also discover that we were never as separate as we thought. Good conversation connects us at a deeper level. As we share our different human experiences, we rediscover a sense of unity. We remember we are part of a greater whole. And as an added joy, we also discover our collective wisdom. We suddenly see how wise we can be together.

For conversation to take us into this deeper realm, I believe we have to practice several new behaviors. Here are the principles I've learned to emphasize before we begin a formal conversation process:

we acknowledge one another as equals

we try to stay curious about each other

we recognize that we need each other's help to become better listeners

we slow down so we have time to think and reflect

we remember that conversation is the natural way humans think together

we expect it to be messy at times

I'd like to describe each of these behaviors in more detail.

We acknowledge one another as equals. **Conversation is an opportunity to meet together as peers, not as roles. What makes us equal is that we're human beings. A second thing that makes us equal is that we need each other. Whatever we know, it is not sufficient. We can't see enough of the whole. We can't figure it out alone. Somebody sees something that the rest of us might need.**

We try to stay curious about each other. **When we begin a conversation with this humility, it helps us be interested in who's there. Curiosity is a great help to good conversation. It's easier for us to tell our story, to share our dreams and fears, when we feel others are genuinely curious about us. Curiosity helps us discard our mask and let down our guard. It creates a spaciousness that is rare in other interactions. It takes time to create this space, but as we feel it growing, we speak more truthfully and the conversation moves into what's real.**

When I'm in conversation, I try to maintain curiosity by reminding myself that everyone here has something to teach me. When they're saying things I disagree with, or have never thought about, or that I consider foolish or wrong, I silently remind myself that they have something to teach me. Somehow this little reminder helps me be more attentive and less judgmental. It helps me stay open to people, rather than shut them out.

We recognize that we need each other's help to become better listeners. I think that the greatest barrier to good conversation is that we've lost the capacity to listen. We're too busy, too certain, too stressed. We don't have time to listen. We just keep rushing past each other. This is true almost everywhere these days. One gift of conversation is that it helps us become good listeners again.

When I'm hosting a conversation, I ask everyone to listen as best they can, and to help each other listen better. We consciously agree on this as part of our purpose for being together. In making this agreement, we are acknowledging that it's hard work to learn how to listen, and that we're all struggling with it. If we talk about this at the start, it makes things easier. If someone hasn't been listening to us, or misinterpreted what we just said, we're less likely to blame that person. We can be a little gentler with the difficulties we experience as we try to become good listeners. And of course, we can't learn to be a good listener alone. We need each other if we're going to learn this skill.

We slow down so we have time to think and reflect. Listening is one of the skills required for good conversation. Slowing down is a second. Most of us work in places where we don't have time to sit together and think. We rush in and out of meetings where we make hurried, not thoughtful, decisions. Conversation creates the conditions for us to rediscover the joy of thinking together. There are different techniques for slowing down the conversation. One, the talking piece, has been adapted from Native American tribal practices. These techniques are well-described in the works cited at the end of this book.

We remember that conversation is the natural way humans think together. **In conversation we are remembering perhaps as much as we are learning. Human beings know how to talk to each other—we've been doing this ever since we developed language. We're not inventing conversation in the 21st century, we're reclaiming it from earlier human experience. Humberto Maturana, a wise Chilean biologist, believes that humans developed language as they moved into family groups and wanted to be more intimate. Language gives us the means to know each other better. That's why we invented it.**

If you're hosting a conversation, you can rely on this history. **We humans know how to do this. It does, however, take time to let go of our modern ways of being in meetings, to get past the behaviors that keep us apart. We've cultivated a lot of bad behaviors when we're together—speaking too fast, interrupting others, monopolizing the time, giving speeches or pronouncements. Many of us have been rewarded for these behaviors. We've become more powerful through their use. But none of these lead to wise thinking or healthy relationships. They only drive us away from each other.**

We expect it to be messy at times. **Because conversation is the natural way that humans think together, it is, like all life, messy. Life doesn't move in straight lines and neither does a good conversation. When a conversation begins, people always say things that don't connect. What's important at the start is that everyone's voice gets heard, that everyone feels invited into the conversation. Everyone will speak from their unique perspective. Thus, they won't say the same things, at all. It can feel as if you're watching a ping pong ball bouncing off a wall as the conversation veers from one topic to another. If you're hosting the conversation, you may feel responsible to draw connections between these diverse contributions (even when you don't see them).**

It's important to let go of that impulse and just sit with the messiness. Each person's contribution adds a different element or spice to the whole. If we connect these too early, we lose the variety we need. If we look for superficial commonalties, we never discover the collective wisdom found only in the depths. We have to be willing to listen, curious about the diversity of experiences and ideas. We don't have to make sense of it right away.

This messy stage doesn't last forever, although it can feel like that. But if we suppress the messiness at the beginning, it will find us later on, and then it will be disruptive. Meaningful conversations depend on our willingness to forget about neat thoughts, clear categories, narrow roles. Messiness has its place. We need it anytime we want better thinking or richer relationships. The first stage is to try and listen well to whatever is being said. Eventually, we will be surprised by how much we share in common. The deeper order that unifies our experience will show itself, but only if we allow chaos early on.

The practice of conversation takes courage, faith, and time. We don't get it right the first time, and we don't have to. We settle into conversation, we don't just do it. As we risk talking to each other about something we care about, as we become curious about each other, as we slow things down, gradually we remember this timeless way of being together. Our rushed and thoughtless behaviors fade away, and we sit quietly in the gift of being together, just as we have always done.

willing to be disturbed

As we work together to restore hope to the future, we need to include a new and strange ally—our willingness to be disturbed. Our willingness to have our beliefs and ideas challenged by what others think. No one person or perspective can give us the answers we need to the problems of today. Paradoxically, we can only find those answers by admitting we don't know. We have to be willing to let go of our certainty and expect ourselves to be confused for a time.

We weren't trained to admit we don't know. Most of us were taught to sound certain and confident, to state our opinion as if it were true. We haven't been rewarded for being confused. Or for asking more questions rather than giving quick answers. We've also spent many years listening to others mainly to determine whether we agree with them or not. We don't have time or interest to sit and listen to those who think differently than we do.

But the world now is quite perplexing. We no longer live in those sweet, slow days when life felt predictable, when we actually knew what to do next. We live in a complex world, we often don't know what's going on, and we won't be able to understand its complexity unless we spend more time in not knowing.

It is very difficult to give up our certainties—our positions, our beliefs, our explanations. These help define us; they lie at the heart of our personal identity. Yet I believe we will succeed in changing this world only if we can think and work together in new ways. Curiosity is what we need. We don't have to let go of what we believe, but we do need to be curious about what someone else believes. We do need to acknowledge that their way of interpreting the world might be essential to our survival.

We live in a dense and tangled global system. Because we live in different parts of this complexity, and because no two people are physically identical, we each experience life differently. It's impossible for any two people to ever see things exactly the same. You can test this out for yourself. Take any event that you've shared with others (a speech, a movie, a current event, a major problem) and ask your colleagues and friends to describe their interpretation of that event. I think you'll be amazed at how many different explanations you'll hear. Once you get a sense of the diversity, try asking even more colleagues. You'll end up with a rich tapestry of interpretations that are much more interesting than any single one.

To be curious about how someone else interprets things, we have to be willing to admit that we're not capable of figuring things out alone. If our solutions don't work as well as we want them to, if our explanations of why something happened don't feel sufficient, it's time to begin asking others about what they see and think. When so many interpretations are available, I can't understand why we would be satisfied with superficial conversations where we pretend to agree with one another.

There are many ways to sit and listen for the differences. Lately, I've been listening for what surprises me. What did I just hear that startled me? This isn't easy—I'm accustomed to sitting there nodding my head to those saying things I agree with. But when I notice what surprises me, I'm able to see my own views more clearly, including my beliefs and assumptions.

Noticing what surprises and disturbs me has been a very useful way to see invisible beliefs. If what you say surprises me, I must have been assuming something else was true. If what you say disturbs me, I must believe something contrary to you. My shock at your position exposes my own position. When I hear myself saying, "How could anyone believe something like that?" a light comes on for me to see my own beliefs. These moments are great gifts. If I can see my beliefs and assumptions, I can decide whether I still value them.

I hope you'll begin a conversation, listening for what's new. Listen as best you can for what's different, for what surprises you. See if this practice helps you learn something new. Notice whether you develop a better relationship with the person you're talking with. If you try this with several people, you might find yourself laughing in delight as you realize how many unique ways there are to be human.

We have the opportunity many times a day, everyday, to be the one who listens to others, curious rather than certain. But the greatest benefit of all is that listening moves us closer. When we listen with less judgment, we always develop better relationship with each other. It's not differences that divide us. It's our judgments about each other that do. Curiosity and good listening bring us back together.

Sometimes we hesitate to listen for differences because we don't want to change. We're comfortable with our lives, and if we listened to anyone who raised questions, we'd have to get engaged in changing things. If we don't listen, things can stay as they are and we won't have to expend any energy. But most of us do see things in our life or in the world that we would like to be different. If that's true, we have to listen more, not less. And we have to be willing to move into the very uncomfortable place of uncertainty.

We can't be creative if we refuse to be confused. Change always starts with confusion; cherished interpretations must dissolve to make way for the new. Of course it's scary to give up what we know, but the abyss is where newness lives. Great ideas and inventions miraculously appear in the space of not knowing. If we can move through the fear and enter the abyss, we are rewarded greatly. We rediscover we're creative.

As the world grows more strange and puzzling and difficult, I don't believe most of us want to keep struggling through it alone. I can't know what to do from my own narrow perspective. I know I need a better understanding of what's going on. I want to sit down with you and talk about all the frightening and hopeful things I observe, and listen to what frightens you and gives you hope. I need new ideas and solutions for the problems I care about. I know I need to talk to you to discover those. I need to learn to value your perspective, and I want you to value mine. I expect to be disturbed by what I hear from you. I know we don't have to agree with each other in order to think well together. There is no need for us to be joined at the head. We are joined by our human hearts.

We never know who we are
Margaret Wheatley

We never know who we are
(this is strange, isn't it?)

or what vows we made
or who we knew

or what we hoped for
or where we were

when the world's dreams
were seeded.

Until the day just one of us

sighs a gentle longing
and we all feel the change

one of us calls a name
and we all know to be there

one of us tells a dream
and we all breath life into it

one of us asks "why?"
and we all know the answer.

It is very strange.

We never know who we are.

part two

a place to pause and reflect

Conversation is the

natural way we humans think together.

We can't be creative if we refuse

to be confused.

It's not differences that divide us.
It's our judgements
about each other that do.

There is no power for change greater than a

community discovering what it cares about.

Am I becoming someone I respect?

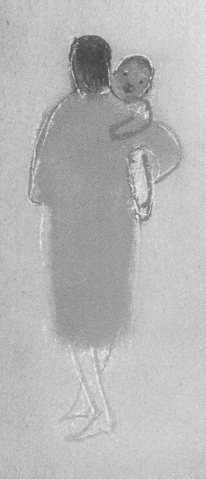

Reality doesn't change itself.
We need to act.

part three

conversation starters

now it's your turn

The first part of this book was written in the hope that you would feel encouraged and even excited to begin conversations. In this section, Part Three, you will find ten conversation starters. Everything in this section is offered to you as a resource for conversations that you will host. Each conversation starter is a short essay framed around a question, and supported by stories, quotes, poems, and my own comments.

But the work is now yours to do. Nothing much will change in the world if you keep these conversation starters to yourself. I hope you will find them provocative enough to share them with friends and colleagues. Indeed, *I hope you will now be the conversation starter*.

I encourage you to begin a conversation with whatever issue or dream is most relevant to you and your friends. But I also hope that you will, either now or later, try out these specific conversation starters. I expect you'll be surprised by the quality and depth of conversation they create. I know you'll be surprised at how easy it is to move into rich and meaningful conversations. And I hope you'll be inspired and surprised by what you learn from your conversation partners.

Please start where you feel most comfortable, and with those who are eager to begin. Gradually, you can expand who's in the conversation, and grow into a more diverse and interesting group. One question to ask of your conversation circle is: Who else should be here? If you ask this question periodically, you will keep noticing others who can contribute new and important elements to your conversation.

New voices revive our energy, and oftentimes help us discover solutions to problems that seem unsolvable. If your conversation circle is stuck, or getting bored, or becoming short-tempered, open the gates and bring in new people. I work from the principle that if we want to change the conversation, we have to change who's in the conversation.

I hope that you will start small and simple, and then occasionally look up and discover others who want to be in conversation with you. I hope that as your conversations progress, you will experience what I have found to be true, that there is no power for change greater than that of a community discovering what it cares about.

Now it's time for you to begin the conversation.

Do I feel a

vocation to be fully human?

We don't set out to save the
world; we set out to wonder how
other people are doing and to
reflect on how our actions affect
other people's hearts.
Pema Chödrön

Do I feel a vocation to be fully human?

Paulo Freire was a Brazilian and world educator who believed in people. Many times he stated that we have "a vocation to be fully human." He demonstrated that when poor and illiterate people learned to think, they could understand what was causing their poverty. Once they understood this, they then acted powerfully to change their world. His approach to education has been called a "pedagogy of love." But what does he mean that we have a vocation to be fully human?

The notion of *vocation* comes from spiritual and philosophical traditions. It describes a "call," work that is given to us, that we are meant to do. We don't decide what our vocation is, we receive it. It always originates from outside us. Therefore, we can't talk about vocation or a calling without acknowledging that there is something going on beyond our narrow sense of self. It helps remind us that there's more than just me, that we're part of a larger and purpose-filled place.

Even if we don't use the word *vocation*, most of us want to experience a sense of purpose to our lives. From a young age, and especially as we mature, people often express the feeling of life working through them, of believing there's a reason for their existence. I always love to hear a young person say that they know there's a reason why they're here. I know that if they can hold onto that sense of purpose, they'll be able to deal with whatever life experiences await them. If we don't feel there's a meaning to our lives, life's difficulties can easily overwhelm and discourage us.

This sense of a purpose beyond ourselves is a universal human experience, no matter our life circumstance. We don't have to be comfortable, well-fed, or safe in order to feel purpose in our lives. Often those in the most terrible circumstances of imprisonment or poverty are the best teachers. How they endure tragedy and suffering gives us the clearest insight into what it means to have a vocation to be fully human.

I was told the story of a pregnant Rwandan mother of six whose village was destroyed by a massacre. She was shot first, buried under the bodies of each of her six slain children, and left for dead. She dug herself out, buried her children, bore her new child, and, soon thereafter, chose to adopt five children whose parents had been killed in the same massacre. She expressed her belief that her life had been spared so that she might care for these orphaned children after losing her own.

This young African mother teaches me what it means to have a vocation to be fully human. I believe we become more fully human with any gesture of generosity, any time we reach out to another rather than withdraw into our individual suffering. To become fully human we need to keep opening our hearts, no matter what. At this time when suffering and anxiety continue to increase, when there is always reason to weep for some unbearable tragedy inflicted by one human on another, I try to remember to keep my heart open.

In my own experience, I notice that I like myself better when I am generous and open-hearted. I don't like who I become when I'm afraid of others, or angry at them. There are many people whose actions anger me and make me afraid—but I don't like how I feel when I respond to them from fear. At those times, I don't feel more human, but less. I become more fully human only when I extend myself. This is how I define for myself what it means to have a vocation to be fully human.

Self-Portrait
    David Whyte

It doesn't interest me if there is one God
or many gods.
I want to know if you belong or feel
abandoned.
If you know despair or can see it in others.
I want to know
if you are prepared to live in the world
with its harsh need
to change you. If you can look back
with firm eyes
saying this is where I stand. I want to know
if you know
how to melt into that fierce heat of living
falling toward
the center of your longing. I want to know
if you are willing
to live, day by day, with the consequence of love
and the bitter
unwanted passion of your sure defeat.

I have heard, in *that* fierce embrace, even
the gods speak of God.

What is my faith

in the future?

What if we discover that our
present way of life is
irreconcilable with our vocation
to become fully human?
Paulo Freire

What is my faith in the future?

Where does the future come from? It often feels these days as if the future arrives from nowhere. Suddenly things feel unfamiliar, we're behaving differently, the world doesn't work the way it used to. We're surprised to find ourselves in this new place—it's uncomfortable, and we don't like it.

The future doesn't take form irrationally, even though it feels that way. The future comes from where we are now. It materializes from the actions, values, and beliefs we're practicing now. We're creating the future everyday, by what we choose to do. If we want a different future, we have to take responsibility for what we are doing in the present.

I have faith in the future because I know it's not a predetermined path we're obligated to walk down. We can change direction from here. It requires critical thinking. We need to look thoughtfully at what's going on, and decide what we want to do about it. Luckily, critical thinking is a skill easy to develop in all people. In Paulo Freire's work with economically poor people, they became skilled thinkers when they saw how reading and analysis would give them the means to fight back against their poverty. People learn quickly when learning offers them the possibility of a better life.

I believe that no matter our life situation, many of us have lost faith in the future. Whether we are economically poor, or leading lives of material advantage that feel meaningless, it is time for us to notice whether we feel hopeful about the future. There is much suffering in the world, and it is increasing. Although these sufferings are not equal (I am not equating a meaningless life with the suffering caused by hunger or violence), this is a painful time for many. If we realize that suffering is common to the human condition, we could begin listening to each other for this shared experience. It would open our hearts to each other, and this would be a good start.

Sometimes we confront the pain of the present and counter it with blind faith. This is especially true in the United States, where it is common to hear statements like: "I have faith in human ingenuity. Whatever the problem is, I know we'll find a solution." This statement is meant to demonstrate the speaker's faith in humanity, and to inspire us. But it fails to acknowledge that, for many serious problems, human ingenuity has already discovered a solution. We aren't lacking solutions. What we lack is the will to implement them.

For example, there are sufficient food and resources to provide for everyone on the planet. What we lack is the political will to use these resources equitably, and to distribute them fairly. The same is true with solutions to many environmental problems, such as too much garbage and not enough places to dump it. There are companies that have nearly zero waste, even though their manufacturing processes use huge quantities of materials. There are also industries that work in concert so that the waste of one becomes the resource of the next (which is how nature does it).

We can't continue to operate from this blind faith in human ingenuity. Our ingenuity has already provided solutions to critical problems. We already know how to create a healthy, life-affirming future for all peoples. We have a different problem—developing the will to act once we know what to do. The gap between knowing and doing is only bridged by the human heart. If we are willing to open our hearts to what's really going on, we will find the energy to become active again. We will find the will and courage to do something. This is true in our individual lives, in our communities and organizations, in our nation-states.

And it is how we can restore hope to the future. It is time for us to notice what's going on, to think about this together, and to make choices about how we will act. We can't keep rejecting solutions because they require us to change our behavior.

We could start by talking about how we feel about what's going on— in our own world, in the greater world. Are we able to live a life that has meaning for us? And to help others live good lives? How do our needs and behaviors affect others—those in our own families, and also in our global family?

If I don't like the life I'm living, then I need to think about why this is so. What's keeping me from being who I want to be? Our individual answers will be different. In an economically prosperous nation, it may be an employer who makes it difficult for me to do what I know is right. In a developing country, it may be lack of employment that keeps me back. It may be cultural beliefs about women or youth that block my way. Some of us are constrained by faceless systems of oppression; some of us are held back by a lack of personal courage. We don't need the same answers, but we all need to be asking the same questions. If we're willing to ask the questions, we can begin changing things.

The future comes from where we are now. The future won't change until we look thoughtfully at our present. We have sufficient human capacities—to think and reflect together, to care about one another, to act courageously, to reclaim the future. These great human capacities moved into action are what give me faith in the future.

from **Mental Fight**
       Ben Okri, Nigeria

What will we choose?
Will we allow ourselves to descend
Into universal chaos and darkness?
A world without hope, without wholeness
Without moorings, without light
Without possibility for mental fight,
A world breeding mass murderers
Energy vampires, serial killers
With minds pining in anomie and amorality
With murder, rape, genocide as normality?

Or will we allow ourselves merely to drift
Into an era of more of the same
An era drained of significance, without shame,
Without wonder or excitement,
Just the same low-grade entertainment,
An era boring and predictable
'Flat, stale, weary and unprofitable'

In which we drift
In which we drift along
Too bored and too passive to care
About what strange realities rear
Their heads in our days and nights,
Till we awake too late to the death of our rights
Too late to do anything
Too late for thinking
About what we have allowed
To take over our lives
While we cruised along in casual flight
Mildly indifferent to storm or sunlight?

Or might we choose to make
This time a waking-up event
A moment of world empowerment?
To pledge, in private, to be more aware
More playful, more tolerant, and more fair
More responsible, more wild, more loving
Awake to our unsuspected powers, more amazing.

We rise or fall by the choice we make
It all depends on the road we take
And the choice and the road each depend
On the light that we have, the light we bend,
On the light we use
Or refuse
On the lies we live by
And from which we die.

What do

I believe about others?

**Love is much more demanding
than law.**
Archbishop Desmond Tutu

What do I believe about others?

We have a great need to rely on the fact of human goodness. Human goodness seems like an outrageous "fact." In these dark times we are confronted daily with mounting evidence of the great harm we so easily do to one another. We are numbed by frequent genocide, ethnic hatred, and acts of violence committed daily in the world. In self-protective groups, we terrorize each other with our hatred. Of the two hundred and forty plus nations in the world, nearly one-fourth of them are at war.

In our daily life, we encounter people who are angry, deceitful, intent only on satisfying their own needs. There is so much anger, distrust, greed, and pettiness that we are losing our capacity to work well together. Many of us are more withdrawn and distrustful than ever. Yet this incessant display of the worst in us makes it essential that we rely on human goodness. Without that belief in each other, there really is no hope.

There is nothing equal to human creativity, human caring, human will. We can be incredibly generous, imaginative, and open-hearted. We can do the impossible, learn and change quickly, and extend instant compassion to those in distress. And these are not behaviors we keep hidden. We exhibit them daily. How often during one day do you figure out an answer to a problem, invent a slightly better way of doing something, or extend yourself to someone in need? Very few people go through their days as dumb robots, doing only repetitive tasks, never noticing that anybody else needs them. Look around at your colleagues and neighbors, and you'll see others acting just like you—people trying to be useful, trying to make some small contribution, trying to help someone else.

But just when we need each other most, we've forgotten who we are. And to make things worse, we're treating one another in ways that bring out our worst. We foster these bad behaviors by treating people in non-human and inhumane ways. We've taken the essential elements of being human—our spirits, our imagination, our need for meaning and for relationships—and dismissed them as unimportant. We've found it more convenient to treat humans as machines, replaceable parts in the economics of production. We've organized work and societies around destructive motivations—greed, self-interest, competition.

After years of being bossed around, of being told they're inferior, of power plays that destroy lives, most people are exhausted, cynical, and focused only on self-protection. Who wouldn't be? These negative and demoralized people have been created by inhumane organizations and governments. People cannot be discounted or used only for someone else's benefit. When obedience and compliance are the primary values, then creativity, commitment, and generosity are destroyed. Whole cultures and generations of people have been deadened by such coercion.

But people's reaction to coercion tells us a great deal about the human spirit. The horrors of the twentieth century showed us the worst of human nature, and the very best. How do you feel when you hear stories of those who wouldn't give in, those who offered compassion to others in the midst of personal horror, those who remained generous in the face of torture and imprisonment? Few of us can hear these stories and remain cynical. We are hungry for these tales—they remind us of what it means to be fully human. We always want more of these stories. We want to be reminded about human goodness.

One of my favorite stories was told to a group of us touring Robben Island, the South African island prison where Nelson Mandela and many others were imprisoned for more than twenty-five years because of their struggle to end apartheid. Their history as prisoners on Robben Island contains many stories of the triumph of the human spirit over torture and severe oppression. My favorite story stands out because it is so unusual.

We were standing in a long narrow room that had been used as a prison cell for dozens of freedom fighters. They lived in close quarters in this barren room—no cots or furniture, just cement walls and floors with narrow windows near the ceiling. We stood there listening to our guide's narration. He had been a prisoner in this very room. The cold came up through the floor into our feet as we gazed around the lifeless cell. We stared through the bars of the door as he described the constant threats and capricious brutality they had suffered. Then he paused and gazed down the length of the room. Speaking very quietly, he said: "Sometimes, to pass the time here, we taught each other ballroom dancing."

I have never forgotten that image, of demoralized and weary men teaching each other to dance in the cold silence of a long prison cell. Only the human spirit is capable of such dancing.

Asking us to notice if we believe in human goodness is not a philosophical question. We will either retreat or move closer together, depending on what we believe about each other. Courageous acts aren't done by people who believe in human badness. Why risk anything if we don't believe in each other? Why stand up for anyone if we don't believe they're worth saving? Who I think you are will determine what I'm willing to do on your behalf. If I believe you're not as good or important as me, I won't even notice you.

Oppression never occurs between equals. Tyranny starts with the belief that some people are more human than others. There is no other way to justify inhumane treatment except to assume that the pain inflicted on the oppressed is not the same as ours. I saw this clearly in South Africa, after apartheid and during the Truth and Reconciliation Commission hearings. In those hearings, white South Africans listened to black mothers grieving the loss of their children to violence, to wives weeping for their tortured husbands, to black maids crying for the children they left behind when they went to work for white families. As the grief of these women and men became public, many white South Africans for the first time saw black South Africans as equally human. In the years of apartheid, they had (consciously or unconsciously) justified their treatment of blacks by assuming that the suffering of blacks was not the same as theirs. They had assumed they were not fully human.

What becomes available to us when we greet each other as fully human? This is an important question as we struggle through this difficult time. We need each other more than ever before. We need everybody's creativity and caring and open hearts to find our way through. We can help one another by trusting that others, too, are fully human. And then we can invite them to step forward with their goodness.

A hopeful future is possible. We can't get there alone, we can't get there without each other, and we can't create it without relying as never before on our fundamental and precious human goodness.

Stars

Margaret Wheatley

In places where air still offers clarity,
stars sing a siren song from space
in the bright night.

Lying on soft earth,
carried into sky by longing,
humans respond to stars
with questions. Why is the Universe
so vast? Why are we so small?

Call and response through the night.

My whole life I have sent
these questions into space. And
listened for response.

Then sky wakens and star song fades.
Humans forget mystery and get on with living.
But the stars, the stars
keep calling. No response.

Why is it that we call to
stars with science and insignificance?

On the next bright night,
find the clear air and ask again.
Humans, ask again. Who are we?
What is our place in mystery?

Perhaps you will hear what I
have heard, a song of inner
radiance.

For the stars
the stars are calling

saying we must
turn to one another
turn to one another and see
finally see
the stars everywhere.

note:
In a clear night sky, for every star we see,
there are 50 million more behind it.

What am I willing to notice

in my world?

How did I get so lucky to have my
heart awakened to others and
their suffering?
Pema Chödrön

What am I willing to notice in my world?

During the winter of 2001, I was in England shortly after a devastating earthquake in India. Daily, the BBC carried photos and descriptions of unbearable suffering, along with interviews with Indians in London whose families lived in areas most affected by the quake. It was a sobering experience, day after day, to listen to the stories and look at the images of horror. During this time, I had dinner with a spiritual leader whose compassion had already led him to India many times to establish orphanages and schools there. These orphanages were unlike traditional orphanages—they were clusters of homes where children lived into adulthood as a community. I was impressed by how much caring had gone into these facilities, and the depth of his love for the people of India.

However, when I began talking about the earthquake, I was surprised when he replied: "I can't deal with it or even think about it. It's just one more overwhelming devastation visited upon a third-world country." I wasn't shocked by the sentiment, but by the words coming from him. How could he work so actively for India, and then close down in the face of this suffering?

I don't know him well enough to ask him that question, but it raises a question for me. What's happening to us as we continue to be bombarded by so much human suffering? What is our coping strategy, conscious or not? I sense that more of us are shutting down. We have no other way of dealing with the haunting faces and frightening images that so frequently appear in our papers and on TV. We turn away, and try to get on with our own lives. Or if the suffering is close to home, we get angry, and want to strike out.

Many times I have fled from others' grief and pain. I've seen this behavior in many others. We don't know how to fix the situation or make the pain go away. There is nothing we can do to help, so we flee in the opposite direction, turn off the television, avert our eyes from the pictures, stop talking to our grieving friends. I don't see these actions helping anyone, even ourselves. It's impossible to shut out the world. We are more aware of what's going on than ever before, and there's no way to change that. As hard as we try to close people out, we never really lose awareness of their suffering. The world still gets in and gnaws at our insides.

The irony is that we want to help, but feel impotent, and so we withdraw the one thing that does help, our companionship. If you've experienced grief, you know how healing it is to just have friends sit with you, not saying a word, not expecting anything from you. You don't need them to do anything except be there, bearing witness to your loss and sorrow.

A few years ago, I was introduced to the practice of "bearing witness." This is not a religious practice. Rather, it's a simple practice of being brave enough to sit with human suffering, to acknowledge it for what it is, to not flee from it. It doesn't make the suffering go away, although it sometimes changes the experience of pain and grief. When I bear witness, I turn toward another and am willing to let their experience enter my heart. I step into the picture by being willing to be open to their experience, to not turn away my gaze.

We are living in a time of increased human sorrow. There is still great poverty, growing hunger, more devastation from disease. There is more warfare, more people on the move seeking refuge in temporary camps. More people devastated by natural disasters of famine, flood, storms, earthquakes.

How we respond to so much suffering is our choice. We can feel hopeless and overwhelmed by this world; we can turn away and just live the best life we can. Or we can learn to bear witness. We can't change the human experience, but we can turn toward, not away from, those struggling. Sometimes I take whatever photo of recent devastation is available from the newspaper—a mother in a refuge camp, a child of war, a family crouched in a shelter—and I just gaze into it, making eye contact, trying to keep my heart open. It's a simple way to keep myself from fleeing from their experience. I can't do much to help, but at least I can link eyes with them, and bear witness to their sorrow. I don't do this to feel better. I do this to keep myself from hiding from the reality of other people's lives.

I've tried other ways to bear witness. Standing and patiently listening to someone I'd rather avoid. Or consciously reading stories of tragedy, torture, massacres—instead of changing channels or turning past the page in the magazine. I used to feel that these horrors were just too much for me to bear. But now I'm learning to read through to the end by reminding myself that I have a role here. If people have survived such atrocities, I honor them by reading about their experiences. They lived it; the least I can do is read about it.

If the world were going along smoothly, if life were growing easier, it wouldn't matter so much which way we were turning. But most of us feel that the world is deteriorating, and we don't expect it to be improving any time soon. Because this is a difficult time for so many, we need a better way to be with hardships and devastation.

We can turn away, or we can turn toward. Those are the only two choices we have.

A Prayer for Children
        Ina J. Hughes
        (an American school teacher),
        adapted by James Steyer

We pray for children
        who sneak popsicles before supper,
        who erase holes in math workbooks,
        who throw tantrums in the grocery store and pick at
                their food,
        who like ghost stories,
        who can never find their shoes.

And we pray for those
        who stare at photographers from behind barbed wire,
        who can't bound down the street in a new pair of sneakers,
        who are born in places we wouldn't be caught dead in,
        who never go to the circus,
        who live in an X-rated world.

We pray for children
        who sleep with the dog and bury the goldfish,
        who bring us sticky kisses and fistfuls of dandelions,
        who get visits from the tooth fairy,
        who hug us in a hurry and forget their lunch money.

And we pray for those
    who never get dessert,
    who have no safe blanket to drag behind them,
    who watch their parents watch them die,
    who can't find any bread to steal,
    who don't have any rooms to clean up,
    whose pictures aren't on anybody's dresser,
    whose monsters are real.

We pray for children
    who spend all their allowance before Tuesday,
    who shove dirty clothes under the bed, and never rinse
    out the tub,
    who don't like to be kissed in front of the carpool,
    who squirm in church or temple and scream in the phone,
    whose tears we sometimes laugh at and
    whose smiles can make us cry.

And we pray for those
    whose nightmares come in the daytime,
    who will eat anything,
    who have never seen a dentist,
    who aren't spoiled by anybody,
    who go to bed hungry and cry themselves to sleep,
    who live and move, but have no being.

We pray for children who want to be carried
    and for those who must,
    for those we never give up on and
    for those who don't get a second chance,
    for those we smother...
    and for those who will grab the hand of anybody kind
    enough to offer it.

When have

I experienced good listening?

Among the Shona people of Zimbabwe,
this is how they greet one another.

"Marare hare?"
Did you sleep?
    "Ndarare kana mararawo."
    I slept well if you slept well.
"Ndarare"
I slept.

        "Makadii?"
        How are you?
    "Ndiripo Makadiwo."
    I am here if you are here.
        "Ndiripo."
        I am here.

When have I experienced good listening?

One of the easiest human acts is also the most healing. Listening to someone. Simply listening. Not advising or coaching, but silently and fully listening.

Whatever life we have experienced, if we can tell someone our story, we find it easier to deal with our circumstances. I have seen the great healing power of good listening so often that I wonder if you've noticed it also. There may have been a time when a friend was telling you such a painful story that you became speechless. You couldn't think of anything to say, so you just sat there, listening closely, but not saying a word. And what was the result of your heartfelt silence, of your listening?

A young, black South African woman taught some of my friends the healing power of listening. She was sitting in a circle of women from many nations, and each woman had the chance to tell a story from her life. When her turn came, she began to quietly tell a story of true horror—of how she had found her grandparents slaughtered in their village. Many of the women were Westerners, and in the presence of such pain they instinctively wanted to do something. They wanted to fix, to make it better, anything to remove the pain of this tragedy from such a young life. The young woman felt their compassion, but also felt them closing in. She put her hands up, as if to push back their desire to help. She said: "I don't need you to fix me. I just need you to listen to me."

She taught many women that day that being listened to is enough. If we can speak our story, and know that others hear it, we are somehow healed by that. During the Truth and Reconciliation Commission hearings in South Africa, many of those who testified to the atrocities they had endured under apartheid would speak of being healed by their own testimony. They knew that many people were listening to their story. One young man who had been blinded when a policeman shot him in the face at close range said: "I feel what... has brought my eyesight back is to come here and tell the story. I feel what has been making me sick all the time is the fact that I couldn't tell my story. But now... It feels like I've got my sight back by coming here and telling you the story."

Why is being heard so healing? I don't know the full answer to that question, but I do know it has something to do with the fact that listening creates relationship. We know from science that nothing in the universe exists as an isolated or independent entity. Everything takes form from relationships, be it subatomic particles sharing energy or ecosystems sharing food. In the web of life, nothing living lives alone.

Our natural state is to be together. Though we keep moving away from each other, we haven't lost the need to be in relationship. Everybody has a story, and everybody wants to tell their story in order to connect. If no one listens, we tell it to ourselves and then we go mad. In the English language, the word for *health* comes from the same root as the word for *whole*. We can't be healthy if we're not in relationship. And *whole* is from the same root word as *holy*.

Listening moves us closer, it helps us become more whole, more healthy, more holy. Not listening creates fragmentation, and fragmentation always causes more suffering. How many teenagers today, in many lands, state that no one listens to them? They feel ignored and discounted, and in pain they turn to each other to create their own subcultures. I've heard two great teachers, Malidoma Somé from Burkino Fasso in West Africa and Parker Palmer from the United States, both make this comment: "You can tell a culture is in trouble when its elders walk across the street to avoid meeting its youth." It is impossible to create a healthy culture if we refuse to meet, and if we refuse to listen. But if we meet, and when we listen, we reweave the world into wholeness. And holiness.

This is a very noisy era. I believe the volume is directly related to our need to be listened to. In public places, in the media, we reward the loudest and most outrageous. People are literally clamoring for attention, and they'll do whatever it takes to be noticed. Things will only get louder until we figure out how to sit down and listen. Most of us would welcome things quieting down. We can do our part to begin lowering the volume by our own willingness to listen.

A school teacher told me how one day a sixteen-year-old became disruptive—shouting angrily, threatening her verbally. She could have called the authorities—there were laws to protect her from such abuse. Instead, she sat down, and asked the student to talk to her. It took some time for him to quiet down; he was very agitated and kept pacing the room. But finally he walked over to her and began talking about his life. She just listened. No one had listened to him in a long time. Her attentive silence gave him space to see himself, to hear himself. She didn't offer advice. She couldn't figure out his life, and she didn't have to. He could do it himself because she had listened.

I love the biblical passage: "Whenever two or more are gathered, I am there." It describes for me the holiness of moments of real listening. The health, wholeness, holiness of a new relationship forming. I have a T-shirt from one conference that reads: "You can't hate someone whose story you know." You don't have to like the story, or even the person telling you their story. But listening creates a relationship. We move closer to one another.

Flawless
   Margaret Wheatley

For far too many years
I have wanted to be flawless,
            Perfecting my pursuits,
            I bargained all for love.

For all these many years
I've made masks of my own doing,
            Pursuing my perfection,
            I found I was pursued.

And then
one day
I fell

            sprawled
            flattened
            lost

on the fertile ground of self.

Naked in dirt
no mask
no bargains
I raised my soiled face
                and there
                you were.

I struggled to stand.

Dirt from my body
clouded your eyes.
Your hand reached
for me.
Blinded,
your
hand
reached
me.

There is, in all of us, a place of pure perfection.
We discover its geography together.

Am I willing to reclaim time

to think?

Sit down and be quiet.
You are drunk, and this is the
edge of the roof.
Rumi

Am I willing to reclaim time to think?

As a species, we humans possess some unique capacities. We can stand apart from what's going on, think about it, question it, imagine it being different. We are also curious. We want to know "why?" We figure out "how?" We think about what's past, we dream forward to the future. We create what we want rather than just accept what is. So far, we're the only species we know that does this.

As the world speeds up, we're giving away these wonderful human capacities. Do you have as much time to think as you did a year ago? When was the last time you spent time reflecting on something important to you? At work, do you have more or less time now to think about what you're doing? Are you encouraged to spend time thinking with colleagues and co-workers, or reflecting on what you're learning?

If we can pause for a moment and see what we're losing as we speed up, I can't imagine that we would continue with this bargain. We're forfeiting the very things that make us human. Our road to hell is being paved with hasty intentions. I hope we can notice what we're losing—in our day-to-day life, in our community, in our world. I hope we'll be brave enough to slow things down.

But I don't expect anybody will give us time to think. We will have to reclaim it for ourselves.

Thinking is the place where intelligent action begins. We pause long enough to look more carefully at a situation, to see more of its character, to think about why it's happening, to notice how it's affecting us and others. Paulo Freire taught critical thinking as a non-violent approach to revolutionary change. He taught poor people how to think about their lives and the forces that were impoverishing them. Nobody believed that exhausted and struggling poor people could become intelligent thinkers. But it is easy for people to develop this capacity when they see how thinking can save their life and the lives of those they love.

Our lives are not as desperate as those poor, and we may not notice that we're losing the possibility of a fully human life. To see whether you're losing anything of value to yourself, here are some questions to ask yourself: Are my relationships with those I love improving or deteriorating? Is my curiosity about the world increasing or decreasing? Do I feel more or less energy for my work than a few years ago? Are those things which anger me different than a few years ago? Which of my behaviors do I value, which do I dislike? Generally, am I feeling more peaceful or more stressed?

If answering those questions helps you notice anything you'd like to change, you will have to find some time to think about it. But don't expect anybody to give you this time. You will have to claim it for yourself.

No one will give it to you because thinking is always dangerous to the status quo. Those benefiting from the present system have no interest in new ideas. In fact, thinking is a threat to them. The moment we start thinking, we'll want to change something. We'll disturb the current situation. We can't expect those few who are well-served by the current reality to give us time to think. If we want anything to change, we are the ones who have to reclaim time.

Thinking is not inaction. When people can think and notice what's going on, we develop ideas that we hope will improve our lives. As soon as we discover something that might work, we act. When the ideas mean something to us, the distance between thinking and acting dissolves. People don't hesitate to get started. They don't sit around figuring out the risks or waiting until someone else develops an implementation strategy. They just start doing. If that action doesn't work, they try something different.

This might sound strange to you, because many of us deal with governments and organizations that can't implement anything. It's true for all bureaucracies—there's a huge gap between ideas and actions. But this is because people don't care about those ideas. They didn't invent them, they know they won't really change anything, and they won't take risks for something they don't believe in. But when it's our idea, and it might truly benefit our lives, then we act immediately on any promising notion.

Determination, courage, genius, and foolishness appear simultaneously when we care deeply about something. Here's how Bernice Johnson Reagon, a gifted singer and songwriter, described her own and other's fearless acts during the Civil Rights Movement. "Now I sit back and look at some of the things we did, and I say, 'What in the world came over us?' But death had nothing to do with what we were doing. If somebody shot us, we would be dead. And when people died, we cried and went to funerals. And we went and did the next thing the next day, because it was really beyond life and death. It was really like sometimes you know what you're supposed to be doing. And when you know what you're supposed to be doing, it's somebody else's job to kill you."

Most of us don't have to risk life and death daily, but we may be dying a slow death. If we feel we're changing in ways we don't like, or seeing things in the world that make us feel sorrowful, then we need time to think about this. We need time to think about what we might do and where we might start to change things. We need time to develop clarity and courage. If we want our world to be different, our first act needs to be reclaiming time to think. Nothing will change for the better until we do that.

from Keeping Still
Pablo Neruda

If we were not so single-minded
about keeping our lives moving,
and for once could do nothing,
perhaps a huge silence
might interrupt this sadness
of never understanding ourselves
and of threatening ourselves with death.

What is the relationship

I want with the earth?

The story of the twentieth century
was finding out just how big
and powerful we were. And it
turns out that we're big and
powerful as all get out. The story
of the twenty-first century is going
to be finding out if we can figure
out ways to get smaller or not.
To see if we can summon the will,
and then the way, to make
ourselves somewhat smaller, and
try to fit back into this planet.
Bill McKibben

What is the relationship I want with the earth?

Other species don't have the same challenge as we humans. They participate with their environment, they watch, they react. We humans, in contrast, dream, plan, figure things out. Because we have consciousness, we create our own set of rules rather than submitting to the laws of nature that govern all life. We use consciousness to try and bend the world to our own purposes. For three centuries now, as Western science has taken control, we've been trying to ignore life's processes rather than respect them. Consciousness has kept us from being in simple partnership with the earth. We've acted as gods rather than as good neighbors.

There is a great deal of well-documented scientific evidence that we're living in an era of unparalleled destruction of species, habitats, and natural resources. Many scientists refer to this time as the sixth great extinction. During its four-to-five billion years of existence, the earth has experienced five earlier massive extinctions. Cycles of destruction are natural to life. But this present destruction is different. It is something we humans created, and it is distinctly unnatural. We created it by using our own rules, rather than those of nature.

Instead of honoring nature's principle of no waste, (one species' waste is always another species' food), we decided we could accumulate huge amounts of garbage. We ignored life's principle of restrained growth, where growth is related to available resources, and instead assumed that the more growth the better. We ignored life's cyclical nature, where decay is the most essential element in a healthy system, and instead assumed we could always be improving, never resting, never ill, hoping to avoid even death. We ignored life's mode of organizing in small, local systems, where small is beautiful, and instead took pride in building the biggest we could, creating gigantic urban sprawls and organizations so large they are unmanageable.

There's a principle in ecology that nature always has the last word. And that's what's happening now. We believed waste could just accumulate, but polluted air and poisoned water are teaching us this is not true. We believed we could grow as large as we dreamed, but the ungovernable nature of huge organizations and the devastated lives of those in mega-cities are teaching us this is not true. We've invested in science to manufacture life to suit ourselves, hoping we might even overcome death, but frightening pandemics and new diseases are teaching us that we live in a web of interconnectedness, and that death is part of life.

We're living in a time when nature offers daily instruction that, while living on earth, it is impossible to live outside of life's fundamental laws and processes. Nature always has the last word. But our rebelliousness up to now has created a bloody mess.

The relationship that we humans have with life is simply expressed by E.O. Wilson, one of the world's great biologists: "If all humanity disappeared, the rest of life (except for pets and house plants) would benefit enormously." Forests would restore themselves, endangered species would slowly recover, and, in general, all life might breathe a sigh of relief that we're gone. However, were any other major species to disappear, for example, ants, the results would be "major extinctions of other species and probably partial collapse of some ecosystems." The whole earth would suffer if it lost any other species except humans.

One of the biggest flaws in our approach to life is the Western belief that competition creates strong and healthy systems. Television screens are filled with images of animals locking horns in battle or ripping apart their prey. It is true that in any living system there are predators and prey, death and destruction. But competition among individuals and species is not the dominant way life works. It is always cooperation that increases over time in a living system. Life becomes stronger and more capable through systems of collaboration and partnering, not through competition.

We aren't often told what happens to ruthless predators, but it's a story we need to know. When a new predator appears in an ecosystem, it acts greedily, consuming far more than its share of available resources. Its greed disturbs the system's balance. Many local species die because their habitat is destroyed. But after a time, the system self-corrects. Either the rapacious species dies off because it has destroyed its food supply and habitat, or it calms down, learns the rules of the neighborhood, and consumes fewer resources. Other local species are able once again to thrive. A healthy ecosystem is always composed of many diverse species living together as a network of cooperation. Each member of the network eats from a specific part of the food web, and leaves the rest for others.

Today, too many of us have forgotten that we live in a web of life. However, the knowledge of our proper role has been held and taught by many indigenous peoples. Their traditional teachings can help us remember that, in this web, we are welcomed as family members, not as greedy consumers.

We have also forgotten that every species is essential to the entire web. We believe we can destroy those species that threaten or annoy us, and no harm will be done anywhere else in the web. We still act surprised when efforts to eliminate one pest end up turning fertile fields into clay or desert, destroying birds, frogs, and thousands of species in the soil, air, and water. We not only kill the pest, we also destroy all those species that are essential to healthy fields.

Life will continue to teach us that we can't make up our own rules. There's only one way to run this planet, and life is pushing back forcefully right now, insisting that we learn this. We are experiencing dramatic and frightening climate changes all around the globe, destructive floods, more deserts and barren soil, new diseases and pandemics. We can't continue to pretend that our modern ways of relating to life are working.

We need to learn how to be good neighbors. I believe the easiest way to become partners with life is to get outside, to be in nature and let her teach us. About half of us no longer have this option. Half of the world's population lives in large cities, breathing polluted air, unable to see the stars, never knowing peace or quiet. I grieve for those of us who cannot know the feel of wild places, the sound of a small stream, the shade of a grove of trees. But for those of us who still have nature available to us, it is even more important that we get outside. We need to experience the power and beauty of life on behalf of all humans who no longer can do this themselves.

On behalf of those who cannot, we need to feel the power of a storm against our faces, the fury of the wind, the cycles of destruction and creation that are always occurring. We need to experience sunlight shining off swamp grasses, to sit with the sunset, to rest under a tree, to go out in the dark and look up to the stars. If we can do these things, we will fall in love with life again. We will become serious about sustaining life rather than destroying it. And our commitment will help all those others who can't ever know what they're missing.

Even Charles Darwin, who interpreted life's evolution as a battlefield of competition, death, and struggle for survival, had paradoxical sensations when he was outdoors in "the smiling fields." He could feel the peace and harmony of the fields, even though his work described warfare. In his journal, he wrote: "It is difficult to believe in the dreadful but quiet war of organic beings, going on in the quiet woods and smiling fields."

If we spent more time outside, letting life teach us, I know we would change our relationship to the earth. We would remember what it feels like to be part of life, rather than trying to play god with it. We would understand the sentiments of Fiona Mitchell, a twenty-two-year-old college student in England who surprised herself by becoming an ecological activist:

I'd love to be able to just get on with my life and enjoy it and do the things I want to do.... And it's really annoying that you can't get on with your life because the planet is being destroyed. But I, personally, can't just ignore it, because it's part of me. It's part of all of us, you know. I think a lot of people don't see the connections between things, the connections that run through everything. We have to take care of everything, because it's all part of the same thing.

Rainer Maria Rilke

You mustn't be frightened
if a sadness
rises in front of you,
larger than any you have ever seen;
if an anxiety,
like light and cloud-shadows,
moves over your hands and over
everything you do.
You must realize that something is
happening to you,
that life has not forgotten you,
that it holds you in its hand
and will not let you fall.

What is my unique contribution

to the whole?

We are different so that we can
know our need of one another, for
no one is ultimately self-sufficient.
A completely self-sufficient person
would be sub-human.
Archbishop Desmond Tutu

If G-d had wanted us to be the same,
He would have created us that way.
The Koran

What is my unique contribution to the whole?

Most cultural traditions have a story to explain why human life is so hard, why there is so much suffering on earth. The story is always the same—at some point early in our human origin, we forgot that we were all connected. We broke apart, we separated from each other. We even fragmented inside ourselves, disconnecting heart from head from spirit. These stories always teach that healing will only be found when we remember our initial unity and reconnect the fragments.

If fragmentation and separation are the problem, how is it possible that our uniqueness could bring us back together? It seems that everywhere we use diversity to further separate from one another. We are organizing against each other, using ethnicity, gender, tightly-bound identities. Even when we aren't warring with each other, we increasingly define ourselves by labels. We stick labels on ourselves, we ask others what theirs are. (Are you a Leo? An ENTJ? An A type personality? A theory Y leader?) We assume we know each other the moment we hear the label. As we become busier, with less time to sit and talk to each other, we increasingly reach for these short-hand identifiers. The result is that we know less about each other, but assume we know more.

But labeling ourselves with minute identities creates far greater tragedy than stereotyping. All around the world, identity is used for self-protection and aggression. Identity has become a weapon; it materializes as campaigns of organized hatred against "others." The twentieth and the early years of the twenty-first century have been filled with the incomprehensible terrors we inflict on one another from fear and hatred. This is what the origin myths predicted—the loss of our humanity from fragmentation and separation. We can't behave as fully human if we believe we're separate.

Very few of us want to continue down the path of separation, or to contribute to more hatred and aggression. If we're going to reweave the world rather than have it disintegrate, we need new ways to understand diversity and differentness. What if we approached each other from our uniqueness?

It's common for people to say that everyone is unique, that no two people are exactly the same. Yet how often do we forfeit our unique self-expression in order to claim an identity? When I identify myself as a white, American, middle-aged woman, of English and German heritage, how adequately does that describe me? These categories may give me a personal sense of location in the world, but over a lifetime, they aren't nearly big enough to describe who I am. And if I restrain my self-expression to keep inside these few categories, I end up feeling constrained and disappointed.

A.R. Ammons, an American poet, expressed this perfectly:

don't establish the
boundaries
first,
the squares, triangles,
boxes
of preconceived
possibility,
and then
pour
life into them, trimming
off left-over edges,
ending potential:

But I alone can't ask to be seen fully for who I am and my unique value. If I want you to acknowledge my gifts, I have to be curious about yours. I have a responsibility to look for and honor yours. We create enough space for our own self-expression only by inviting in everybody else's uniqueness.

Whenever we get past the categories and stereotypes, when we greet each other as interesting individuals, we are always surprised by who we are. I'm sure you've had the experience of stereotyping someone because of their appearance, and then being surprised when they didn't fit that judgment. This has happened to me so often you'd think I wouldn't keep labeling people—a laborer in ill-fitting clothes who talked with me about his love of Shakespeare, a youth with brightly dyed blue hair and body piercings who described his work teaching non-violence to young children, a factory worker who shared her poetry, a desperately poor village woman who invited me in to her immaculate, one-room home. But still I am surprised. When will I be free of these categories that prevent me from enjoying who you are?

Bernie Glassman, co-founder of the Zen Peacemaker Order, says the only thing we have in common is our differences. When we understand that, he says, we discover our oneness. Most of us have had the experience of listening to someone and realizing how different they are from us. We don't share any of their experiences, values, or opinions. But surprisingly, at the end of listening to them, we feel more connected to them.

Bernie tells the story of two people whose past history could have kept them separated by anger and fear forever. He was leading a group to Auschwitz, to bear witness to the death camp and the 1.5 million people killed there. Of the 150 diverse people in the group, two people had great reason to hate one another, the American-born son of a Jewish concentration camp inmate and the German daughter of the Nazi commandant of that same camp:

For many years the American had heard stories from his father about the brutality of the camp commandant, and coming face-to-face with the man's daughter in Auschwitz had been almost intolerable for him. He didn't want to meet or talk to her, he wanted to remain silent. But when the two finally talked and exchanged stories, they discovered they had many things in common, including shame, guilt, and silence. The expected anger of that first meeting eventually evolved into a deep and powerful bond of understanding and empathy, and finally into a strong, meaningful friendship.

Such healing is possible because, in all our diversity, we share the experience of being human. We each have the same longings and feelings. We each feel fear, loneliness, grief. We each want to be happy and to live a meaningful life. We discover this shared human experience whenever we listen to someone's unique story. The details and differences are important to hear. (Nothing shuts down our story faster than someone saying "I know exactly how you feel.") But as we listen quietly to their story, as we allow another's life to be different from ours, suddenly we find ourselves standing on common ground.

In my experience, there is a common human experience, always expressed in richly diverse ways. Here are some of the common longings I've noticed across cultures and traditions.

We want our children to be healthy. We want peace and stability in our lives and communities. We want changes that help relieve suffering. Poor or wealthy, we prefer to be generous and helpful. We want to learn things that are useful to us. We want to know why our life is this way and not otherwise, the meaning of it all.

These common human longings are expressed in millions of different ways. Every difference teaches us something new about the human journey. In Hinduism's Rig Veda, there is the image of Indra's Net. We are all individual jewels that shine uniquely. But we are all jewels gleaming on the same web, each sparkling outward from our place on the net, each reflected in the other. As paradoxical as it is, our unique expressions are the only source of light we have to see each other. We need the light from each unique jewel in order to illuminate our oneness.

Indra's Net
    from the *Rig Veda*
    as described by Anne Adams

There is an endless net of threads throughout
the universe...
At every crossing of the threads there is
an individual.
And every individual is a crystal bead.
And every crystal bead reflects
not only the light from every
other crystal in the net
but also every other reflection
throughout the entire universe.

When have I experienced

working for the common good?

"We didn't save ourselves.
We tried to save each other."
A survivor, World Trade Center,
September 11, 2001.

Life is too short to be selfish.

When have I experienced working for the common good?

For many years, I have talked with people who helped rescue people from disasters—bombings, floods, fires, explosions. They always describe their experiences with grief, yet with energy and satisfaction. It seems strange that, in the face of horror, they have these good feelings. But they're describing an experience of working for the common good—doing whatever is necessary to help another human being. And that experience is always deeply satisfying.

In a crisis, the space is wide open for contribution. There's no time to worry or hesitate, there are few or no rules. People have a deep desire to help, so they perform miracles. We discover capacities we didn't know we had. The chaos and urgency of a disaster encourages people to try anything, far beyond any plan or training. As one person said: "There's no risk, because it's already a disaster. You just keep doing whatever you can to help. If one thing doesn't work, you try something else."

This is the true irony of disasters, especially those created through human acts of violence—they show us how good the majority of people are. Goodness and talent are common human traits. Most people are more generous and talented than we assume. It's hard to see this day-to-day when we work in restrictive environments where we're told what to do, told what to think, usually ignored, often disrespected, sometimes dehumanized. Once you've worked and lived under these conditions, it's difficult to remember your own capacities, let alone those of others. But in an emergency, when others are suffering, we emerge powerfully, leaving behind our roles, our boredom, our exhaustion. Disasters reveal capacities long buried by bureaucracy and disrespect.

You may never have participated directly in a rescue operation, even though all of us have watched them now on global TV. But in our daily lives, most of us have had memorable experiences of working with others, discovering how much talent and goodness were available. It might have been an intense team project, or working with neighbors, or an accident or small crisis—any experience where you worked for others rather than yourself.

How well do you remember that experience? Do you remember the purpose of the work? How often did your efforts teeter on the brink of failure? How many times were you surprised by someone's ingenuity, or your own? And now, long after it's over, how do you feel about those with whom you shared this experience?

When we work for the common good, we experience each other in new ways. We don't worry about differences, or status, or traditional power relationships. We worry about whether we'll succeed in accomplishing what needs to be done. We focus on the work, not on each other. We learn what trust is. We learn the necessity of good communication.

These are always the conditions that bring out our best—we're focused on something we really care about; we work intensely together, inventing solutions as needed; we take all kinds of risks; we communicate constantly.

These experiences give us the chance to change our minds about each other. We can see each other free from the roles and routines that conceal most of who we are. Free from jobs that keep us too busy to notice each other. Free from the fatigue that keeps us too tired to be interested in each other.

It shouldn't take a crisis or disaster to help us learn that goodness and talent are something we hold in common as humans. There are quieter and simpler ways to learn who somebody is, what their talents are, how their life challenges them. For instance, we can sit down and talk with them.

Working for something beyond ourselves teaches us about the human spirit. It's easy to feel hopeful about people after one of these experiences. But when we serve others, we gain more than hope. We gain energy. People who volunteer for a community or service project often arrive straight from work, exhausted. But after several hours of meaningful volunteer work, they go home energized. In disaster relief efforts, people work without rest for days, gaining energy from the work of saving others. Work that serves the common good doesn't take away our energy. Instead, energy pours into our bodies through our open hearts and generous spirits.

Most people describe working for the common good as memorable, and contrast this with their day-to-day work. They refer to their daily jobs as "the real world." The experiences that give them energy and hope are labeled as unique or different. What keeps us from seeing these experiences of human goodness and talent as real? Why do we take what's boring and destructive and call that the real world? How did we develop such poor expectations for what's possible when we work together?

What if we used our experiences of working for the common good as the standard? We would stop tolerating work and lives that gradually dissolve our belief in each other. We might begin to insist on the conditions that bring out our best. If we stopped accepting the deadening quality of "the real world," if we raised our expectations, then it wouldn't take a crisis for us to experience the satisfaction of working together, the joy of doing work that serves other human beings.

And then we would discover, as the Chinese author of the Tao te Ching wrote 2600 years ago, that "the good becomes common as grass."

Tao Te Ching,
   600 B.C. China
   Stephen Mitchell,
   translator

If you want to be a leader...
stop trying to control.
Let go of fixed plans and concepts,
and the world will govern itself.

The more prohibitions you have,
the less virtuous people will be.
The more weapons you have,
the less secure people will be.
The more subsidies you have,
the less self-reliant people will be.

Therefore the Master says:
I let go of the law,
and people become honest.
I let go of economics,
and people become prosperous.
I let go of religion,
and people become serene.
I let go all desire for the common good,
and the good becomes common as grass.

When do I experience

sacred?

I don't know what peace is.
But I love it.
Six-year-old Afghanistan child,
interviewed in a refugee camp,
May 2001.

When do I experience sacred?

I experience sacred as a feeling. It's how I feel when I am open to life. Or am opened by life. Sacred is not a special place, or a ritual, or a particular group of people. It's more normal than that. There are many places and rituals that do feel sacred, and many of us seek these out, myself included. But I think it's important to notice that the ritual isn't sacred, it just opens the door to the experience. It isn't only the place that is sacred, we are.

I find it sad that so many of us have forgotten, or never learned, that sacred is an everyday experience. We've been told we have to wait for the sacred space, or the priest or shaman, or the right sounds and scents. Many traditions and cultures want it to be that way. This is a time-tested way to control people. We are told there is no way to access sacred directly, that we need intermediaries for sacred experience. When we don't know that sacred is available in our day-to-day lives, when we have to wait for somebody else to give us the experience, it is very difficult to know ourselves as sacred. In the absence of that knowledge, we more easily accept domination and the loss of our freedom. When sacred becomes a special rather than common experience, it becomes difficult to feel fully alive and fully human.

Sacred is nothing special. It's just life, revealing its true nature. Life's true nature is wholeness, Indra's net embracing every living thing, able to contain all unique expressions. In a sacred moment, I experience that wholeness. I know I belong here. I don't think about it, I simply feel it. Without any work on my part, my heart opens and my sense of "me" expands. I'm no longer locked inside a small self. I don't feel alone or isolated. I feel here. I feel welcomed.

As I write this, through my window I've noticed a mother bird flying back and forth, worms dangling from her beak. She's working diligently to provide for her babies. Watching her, I remember my own mothering, and suddenly, I feel connected to all other beings who, as mothers, try to keep life going. A brief moment of noticing one hard-working bird, and I feel different, more connected. The bird, me, mothers everywhere, we're all doing our part to bring more life into the world. She does her work, I do mine, and in this moment of recognition, my heart opens to the truth that we all share in this together. Instead of feeling tired by such responsibility, I feel blessed.

I described sacred as the feeling that I belong here. If this is true for others, it would explain why people everywhere are mourning the loss of community. We are suffering from living in a fragmented state. Separated from each other, cut off from nature, we can't experience sacred. And I think we know what we're missing. We know we're missing the richest experience of being human, the inexplicable mixture of feelings that can never be described well. "I felt joy, yet I was crying. I felt peaceful, yet very energized. I felt like me, but I was more than me."

In your own experience, how would you describe sacred? If you can recall times that felt sacred to you, was there a sense of feeling connected to something beyond yourself? Did you experience yourself in a different, perhaps larger way? Sometimes we have this feeling when we gaze at a newborn child. Or sit by quiet water. Or look up to see someone smiling at us. Or respond to music, or a storm, or anything whose beauty catches us by surprise. How would you describe the feeling of sacred?

We can't experience sacred in isolation. It is always an experience of connecting. It doesn't have to be another person. (Remember, I just connected with a bird.) It can be a connection with an idea, a feeling, an object, a tradition. The connection moves us outside ourselves into something greater. Because we move out beyond ourselves, the experience of sacred is often described as spacious, open, liberating. We learn that we are larger than we thought.

We also learn, in these moments, that life is not to be feared. Sacred experiences always offer gentle reassurance that everything is all right, just as it is. People describe this awareness as surrender, or acceptance, or grace. If only for a moment, we let down our guard and experience life undefended. Defenseless, we feel peace. I hope that you have had this experience many times in your life. I find it important to keep recalling these brief moments of peace. They help me remember that peace is available, no matter what circumstance I'm in.

In this turbulent time, we crave connection; we long for peace;
we want the means to walk through the chaos intact. We are seeking
things that are only available through an experience of sacred. Yet
sometimes in pursuit of these goals we flee from people and withdraw
into an environment we think we can control. Or we blot out our
longings with mind-numbing experiences or substances. But we cannot
find connection, community, and peace by withdrawing from others
or going unconscious. The peace we seek is found in experiencing
ourselves as part of something bigger and wiser than our little, crazed
self. The community we belong to is all of life. The turbulence cannot
be controlled, but when we stop struggling and accept it as part of
life, it feels different.

Sacred experiences give us what we need to live in this strange yet
wondrous time. We need as many sacred moments as we can find.
We invite these moments when we open to life and to each other.
In those grace-filled moments of greeting, we know we're part of all
this, and that it's all right.

Canyon Days
A week in Moqui Canyon, Lake Powell
       Margaret Wheatley

In morning, ravens call
the canyon into dawn.

They pluck raucous echoes
from red rocks,
sounds my children
plant there the night before.

At night, the moon bleaches
my hair, and planes at 37,000 feet
leave silver contrails,
comet tails too hurried to bend
to Earth's easy curve.

This morning I can't find
my truck.
Ravens sit on boat trailers, muttering.
"Raven, help me find my car,"
I ask, and walk on faithless.
I turn and find my car.
Raven on the hood flies off.

Tonight, moon bride,
I dress in white.
Water plays jug band
rhythm as I swoon into the sky.
Me and these stars,
no time, no distance,
swaying to the music
in our canyon home.

gestures of love

Only love is big enough to hold all the pain of this world.
Sharon Salzberg

I hope now, at the end of this book, that you've started a few conversations. If you have, I wonder if you've experienced them as gestures of love.

I think of a gesture of love as anything we do that helps others discover their humanity. Any act where we turn to one another. Open our hearts. Extend ourselves. Listen. Any time we're patient. Curious. Quiet. Engaged.

Earlier in these pages, I offered my own description of what it means to have a vocation to be fully human. I feel we become more fully human through our generosity, when we extend to another rather than withdraw into ourselves.

Conversation does this—it requires that we extend ourselves, that we open our minds and hearts a bit more, that we turn to someone, curious about how they live their life. I hope you've had these experiences in conversation.

Speaking to each other involves risk. It's often difficult to extend ourselves, to let down our guard, especially with those we fear or avoid. When we're willing to overcome our fear and speak to them, that is a gesture of love. Strangely, what we say is not that important. We have ended the silence that keeps us apart.

I learned this listening to Bernie Glassman describe a meeting between two homeless men. One was a "mole person." He lived underground in New York City, with thousands of other homeless people who never come up to the streets. The other man lived in city parks. Bernie described his delight when these two reclusive and withdrawn men began talking to each other. A woman questioned whether there was any value in this conversation—the men seemingly had spoken more lies than truth. Bernie quickly replied: "It doesn't matter what they were saying. They were talking to each other."

I think about how much courage it took for those two frightened men to speak. Bernie knew the courage of their actions, the first tentative extension out from their painful, private experience. He wasn't concerned with their words. (And he knew that if they kept talking, they'd gradually become more truthful—for this is what always happens.)

Paulo Freire described love as "an act of courage, not of fear." When we find the courage to approach those we fear, that is a gesture of love.

When we're brave enough to risk a conversation, we have the chance to rediscover what it means to be human. In conversation, we practice good human behaviors. We think, we laugh, we cry, we tell stories of our day. We become visible to one another. We gain insights and new understandings. And as we stay in conversation, we may discover that we want to be activists in our world. We get interested in what we can do to change things. Conversation wakes us up. We no longer accept being treated poorly. We become people who work to change our situation.

Conversation helps us reclaim these very human capacities and experiences. That is a gesture of love.

This may sound strange, but conversation is the practice of freedom. As we think together, as we question things, as we are stirred to act to change things, we exercise our innate right to be free. Freire said that a genuine act of love always generates "other acts of freedom; otherwise, it is not love." So freedom and love are intimately related. When our actions create freedom for ourselves and others, that too is a gesture of love.

Conversation can only take place among equals. If anyone feels superior, it destroys conversation. Words then are used to dominate, coerce, manipulate. Those who act superior can't help but treat others as objects to accomplish their causes and plans. When we see each other as equals, we stop misusing them. We are equal because we are human beings. Acknowledging you as my equal is a gesture of love.

What happens when we claim our right to be fully human? Everyone benefits. Even those who feel superior, who demean and discount us, benefit when we claim our full humanity. When we refuse to accept degrading conditions and behaviors, those in power no longer have a target for their oppressive acts. Even if they want to continue in their old ways, we don't let them. Our refusal gives them the opportunity to explore new, more humane behaviors. They may not choose to change, but as we stand up for ourselves, we give them the chance to be more fully human as well. When we are courageous enough to honor ourselves, we offer everyone else their humanity.

It's a wonderful realization—claiming our vocation to be fully human is the way we extend love to all others. As such, it is the ultimate gesture of love.

Sister Helen Kelley

Choose Life
only that and always,
and at whatever risk.
To let life leak out, to let it wear away by
the mere passage of time, to withhold
giving it and spreading it
is to choose
nothing.

turning to one another

There is no power greater than a community discovering what it cares about

Ask "What's possible?" not "What's wrong?" Keep asking.

Notice what you care about.
Assume that many others share your dreams.

Be brave enough to start a conversation that matters.
 Talk to people you know.
 Talk to people you don't know.
 Talk to people you never talk to.

Be intrigued by the differences you hear.
 Expect to be surprised.
 Treasure curiosity more than certainty.

Invite in everybody who cares to work on what's possible.
 Acknowledge that everyone is an expert about something.
 Know that creative solutions come from new connections.

Remember, you don't fear people whose story you know.
Real listening always brings people closer together.

Trust that meaningful conversations can change your world.

Rely on human goodness. Stay together.

referenced quotes

vii. "You must give birth…" adapted from Rilke, *Letters to a Young Poet*.

4. "Archbishop Desmond Tutu describes it…" in Tutu, p. 212.

5. "As sociologist John Berger describes it…" in McLaren, p. 18.

26. "Paulo Freire, a Brazilian and world educator who used education…" in Freire, *Pedagogy of the Oppressed*, p. 123.

57. "We don't set out to change the world…" in Chödrön, *When Things Fall Apart*, p. 100.

58. "His approach to education has been called a 'pedagogy of love.'" in McLaren.

63. "What if we discover that our present way of life is…" in Freire, *Pedagogy of the Oppressed*, p. 61.

71. "Love is much more demanding…" in Tutu, p. 75.

72. "Of the 240 or so nations…" see "Downward Trend in Armed Conflicts Reversed" by A.J. Jongman www.fsw.leidenuniv.nl

79. "How did I get so lucky…" Pema Chödrön, Omega, New York, May 1999.

89. "I feel what has been making me sick…" in Tutu, p. 128.

99. "Here's how Bernice Johnson Reagon…" in Salzberg, p. 151.

103. "The story of the twentieth century was…" in Suzuki, p. 275.

106. "If all humanity disappeared…" in Suzuki, p. 13-14.

109. "We would understand the sentiments of…" in Suzuki, p. 272.

111. from Letters to a *Young Poet*, p. 92-93

113. "We are different so that…" in Tutu, p. 214.

113. "If G-d had wanted us…" Imam Makram El-Amin, at Minneapolis Interfaith Dialogue, May 9, 2001.

116. "A.R. Ammons, an American poet…" in *Tape for the Turn of the Year*, p. 116.

118. "For many years the American had heard…" in Glassman, p. 28.

120. Indra's net, as described by Anne Adams, from the *Rig Veda*.

138. "Only love is big enough…" in Salzberg, p. 109.

140. "Paulo Freire described love as…" in Freire, *Pedagogy of the Oppressed*, p. 78.

140. "Freire said that a genuine act of love…" in Freire, *Pedagogy of the Oppressed*, p. 78.

credits and permissions

Poems

From *The Tao Te Ching*, by Lao Tzu,
translated by Stephen Mitchell, Section 57
"If you want to be a great leader..."
©1988, by Stephen Mitchell. Reprinted by
permission of HarperCollins Publishers, Inc.,
and Pan MacMillan Ltd.

"Self-Portrait" from *Fire in the Earth*,
by David Whyte. ©1992, by David Whyte.
Reprinted by permission of David Whyte.

From *Mental Fight* by Ben Okri:
©1999, by Ben Okri. Reprinted by permission
of David Godwin Associates on behalf of the
author.

"For the Children" from *Turtle Island*
by Gary Snyder. ©1974, by Gary Snyder.
Reprinted by permission of New Directions
Publishing Corp.

Photos

Opening photo: Latvian family, Riga.
©Jim Brandenburg, used with permission
of Minden Pictures.

Closing photo: Cham women returning from
market, Indochina 1952 (Vietnam/Cambodia).
©Werner Bischof, used with permission
of Magnum Photos.

bibliography

Abram, David. *The Spell of the Sensuous: Perception and Language in a More Than Human World.* New York: Vintage Books, 1997.

Ammons, A.R. *Tape for the Turn of the Year.* New York: W.W. Norton Co., 1965.

Arrien, Angeles. *The Four-Fold Way: Walking the Paths of the Warrior, Teacher, Healer and Visionary.* San Francisco: HarperSan Francisco, 1993.

Baldwin, Christina. *Calling the Circle, The First and Future Culture.* New York: Bantam, 1997.

_____, *The Seven Whispers: Listening to the Voice of Spirit.* Novato, California: New World Library, 2002. (forthcoming)

Bender, Sue. *Everyday Sacred: A Woman's Journey Home.* New York: HarperCollins, 1995.

Bernard, Ted, and Jora M. Young. *The Ecology of Hope: Communities Collaborate for Sustainability.* Gabriola Island, B.C.: New Society Publishers, 1996.

Block, Peter. *The Answer to How is Yes: Acting on What Matters.* San Francisco: Berrett-Koehler Publishers, 2002.

Chödrön, Pema. *When Things Fall Apart.* Boston: Shambhala Publications Inc., 1997.

Chödrön, Pema. *The Places that Scare You: A Guide to Fearlessness in Difficult Times.* Boston: Shambhala Publications Inc., 2001.

Freire, Paulo. *Pedagogy of the Oppressed.* New York: Herder and Herder, 1970.

_____. *Education for Critical Consciousness.* (Myra B. Ramos, trans.) New York: Continuum, 1973.

Glassman, Bernie. *Bearing Witness: A Zen Master's Lessons in Making Peace.* New York: Bell Tower, 1998.

Halamandaris, Val J. *Great Secrets of the Universe: A Compendium of Caring Thought.* Washington, D.C.: Caring Publishing, 2000.

Hawkins, Paul. *The Ecology of Commerce.* New York: HarperCollins, 1993.

Jongman, A.J. "Downward Trend in Armed Conflicts Reversed" at www.fsw.leidenuniv.nl

Kemmis, Daniel. *Community and the Politics of Place.* Oklahoma: University of Oklahoma Press, 1992.

Kretzman, B., and J. McKnight. *Building Communities from the Inside Out: A Path Towards Finding and Mobilizing a Community's Assets.* Chicago: ACTA Publications, 1997.

Kellert, Stephen, and Edward O. Wilson, editors. *The Biophylia Hypothesis.* Washington D.C.: Island Press, 1993.

Laszlo, Ervin. *Macroshift: Navigating the Transformation to a Sustainable World.* San Francisco: Berrett-Koehler Publishers, 2001.

Leakey, Richard, and Roger Lewin. *The Sixth Extinction: Patterns of Life and the Future of Humankind.* New York: Anchor Books, 1997.

Loeb, Paul Rogat. *Soul of a Citizen: Living with Conviction in a Cynical Time.* New York: St. Martin's Press, 1999.

Lusseyran, Jacques. *And There Was Light.* New York: Parabola Books, 1998.

Macy, Joanna, and Molly Young Brown. *Coming Back to Life: Practices to Reconnect Our Lives, Our World.* Canada and USA: New Society Publishers, 1998.

McKnight, John. *The Careless Society: Community and its Counterfeits.* New York: Basic Books, 1995.

McLaren, Peter. *Paulo Freire and Che Guavara, and The Pedagogy of Revolution.* Lanham, Maryland: Rowman & Littlefield Publishers, Inc., 2000.

Mitchell, Steven. *Tao Te Ching.* New York: HarperPerennial, 1992.

Morley, Barry. *Beyond Consensus: Salvaging Sense of the Meeting.* Wallingford, Pennsylvania: Pendle Hill Pamphlet 307.

Neruda, Pablo. *Extravagaria.* Alistair Reid, trans. New York: Noonday Press, 2001.

Okri, Ben. *Mental Fight.* London: Phoenix Books, 1999.

Palmer, Parker. *Let Your Life Speak: Listening for the Voice of Vocation.* San Francisco: Jossey-Bass, Inc., 2000.

Palmer, Parker. *The Courage to Teach.* San Francisco: Jossey-Bass, Inc., 1998.

Rilke, Rainer Maria. Stephen Mitchell, Trans. *Letters to a Young Poet.* New York: Vintage Books, 1986.

Salzberg, Sharon. *Lovingkindness: The Revolutionary Art of Happiness.* Boston and London: Shambhala Publications, Inc., 1997.

_____. *A Heart as Wide as the World.* Boston: Shambhala Publications, Inc., 1997

Schumacher, E.O. *Small is Beautiful.* New York: Harper & Row, 1973.

Suzuki, David and Holly Dressel. *From Naked Ape to Superspecies.* Toronto: Stoddart, 1999.

Snyder, Gary. *Turtle Island.* New York: New Directions Publishing, 1974.

The Compact Edition of the Oxford English Dictionary. Volume I. Oxford University Press, 1971.

Trout, Susan. *Born to Serve: The Evolution of the Soul Through Service.* Alexandria, Virginia: Three Roses Press, 1997.

Tutu, Desmond Mpilo. *No Future Without Forgiveness.* London: Rider, 1999.

Watkins, Jane Magruder and Bernard J. Mohr. *Appreciative Inquiry: Change at the Speed of Imagination.* San Francisco: Jossey-Bass/Pfeiffer, 2001.

Wright, Robert. *NonZero: The Logic of Human Destiny.* New York: Vintage Books, 2001.

Whyte, David. *Fire in the Earth.* Langley, Washington: Many Rivers Press, 1999.

websites

Listed here are a few websites that relate to one or more of the conversations and issues in *Turning to One Another*. This is far from complete, but I offer it to get you started as you look for more in-depth information on the web.

Appreciative Inquiry Resource List. www.serve.com/taos/appreciative.html

Asset Based Community Development Institute. www.nwu.edu/IPR/abcd.html

Berkana Institute. The institute that I head, focused on life-affirming global leadership. www.berkana.org

Caring Institute, believing that the solution to most problems is found in human caring. www.caring-institute.org

Chaordic Commons, a network for organizations experimenting with new forms to ensure a sustainable world. www.chaord.org

Co-Intelligence Institute, a rich resource of people, processes, and websites that support democracy and intelligent action. www.co-intelligence.org

Cultural Creatives, information about the millions of people who are thinking differently and working for societal change. www.culturalcreatives.org

Ecoliteracy—teaching children how to care for the earth through projects developed in local schools. www.ecoliteracy.org

Emerging (younger) leaders connected as a worldwide network doing hopeful and passionate work. www.pioneersofchange.org

Families around the world, from the book *Families as We Are*: Conversations from Around the World by Perdita Houston www.familiesasweare.com

From The Four Directions, a global leadership initiative of The Berkana Institute. www.fromthefourdirections.org

Future Search, a process for involving the whole community in declaring its vision and moving its dreams into action. www.futuresearch.net

Institute of Noetic Sciences, creating a global wisdom society in which consciousness, spirituality and love are at the center of life. www.noetic.org

Joanna Macy, one of the most compassionate and effective societal change activists in the world. www.joannamacy.net

New Stories (founder, Bob Stilger) online learning communities for colleges and large scale systems change initiatives. Bob is a close friend and colleague, from whom I've learned a great deal. www.newstories.org

Open Space Technology, a powerful process originated by Harrison Owen for self-organized meetings based on people's interests. www.openspaceworld.org

Paulo Freire's work. www.paulofreire.org
In English and Portuguese.

Public Conversation Project, an initiative
to bring conversation processes to difficult
public and community issues.
www.publicconversations.org

Spiritual activism supported by local
conversation circles in the U.S. and
elsewhere. www.renaissancealliance.org

Sustainability in homes, communities,
worksites. Includes the wonderful
commentaries of the late Donella
Meadows. www.sustainer.org

*Turning the Tide: Nine Actions for the
Planet.* Simple ways to make a personal
and powerful difference.
www.newdream.org/turnthetide

Vision for a Better World Foundation.
www.insurancealternatives.com

Zen Peacemaker Order, co-founded
by Bernie Glassman.
www.peacemakercommunity.org/

about the author

Margaret (Meg) Wheatley writes, teaches, and speaks about radically new practices and ideas for how we can live together harmoniously in these chaotic times. She has worked for nearly thirty years in organizations of all types, on all continents, and is a committed global citizen. Her aspiration is to help create organizations and communities where people are seen as the blessing, not the problem. She is president of The Berkana Institute, a charitable global foundation supporting life-affirming leaders around the world. Since 2000, Berkana's initiative, "From the Four Directions: People Everywhere Leading the Way," has been organizing conversations among people in their local communities in over thirty countries. These conversation circles have inspired many local leaders to take action in their communities. Berkana supports their activities with many different types of resources. These local leaders also are linked together as a worldwide web of life-affirming leaders. For more information, see www.berkana.org.

Meg has been an organizational consultant since 1973, as well as a professor of management in two graduate business programs. She received her doctorate in organizational behavior from Harvard University, an M.A. in systems thinking from New York University, and has been a research associate at Yale University. She has also been a public school teacher and administrator in inner cities, and a Peace Corps Volunteer in Korea. She has been recognized by several awards and honorary doctorates.

Meg's work appears in two award-winning books, *Leadership and the New Science* (1992, 1999) and *A Simpler Way* 1996), plus many videos and articles. She has drawn many of her ideas from new science and life's ability to organize in self-organizing, systemic, and cooperative modes. And increasingly, her hopes and designs for new organizations are drawn from her understanding of many different cultures and spiritual traditions. Her articles and work can be found at www.margaretwheatley.com.

She lives with gratitude in the peaceful mountains of Utah, while her large family is now spread throughout the United States.

To contact Meg:
The Berkana Institute
P.O. Box 1407
Provo, Utah, 84603, USA
1-801-377-2996
1-801-377-2998 (fax)
info@berkana.org

other work by margaret wheatley

Leadership and the New Science: Discovering Order in a Chaotic World.
Berrett-Koehler Publishers Inc., 1992 and revised edition, 1999.

Interprets and applies discoveries from the new sciences of chaos and complexity theory, quantum physics, and the new biology, to leadership and organizational issues. Named "Best Management Book" of 1992, "Top Ten Business books of the 90s" by CIO Magazine, and "Top Ten Business books of all time" by Xerox Corporation.

Also an award-winning **video** "Leadership and the New Science" from CRM films. Also available as **audiotape**, read by the author.

A Simpler Way (co-author).
Berrett-Koehler Publishers Inc., 1996.

Using prose, poetry, and photos, explores the question: How might we organize human endeavor if we understood how life organizes?

Available as **audiotape**, read by the authors.

Videos
It's a Wonderful Life.
Explores servant leadership using clips from the classic movie starring Jimmy Stewart.

Twelve Angry Men.
The practices of highly effective teams, using the classic movie starring Henry Fonda.

Articles
Many articles, including all current ones, are available for free on the website listed below.

For information on ordering any of these products, **www.margaretwheatley.com**

Two excellent resources for the practice of conversation

Christina Baldwin works through PeerSpirit, Inc., a firm she partners in with Ann Linnea. Their organization teaches circle practice and council management to communities, organizations, and individuals. I find Christina's book, *Calling the Circle, The First and Future Culture* (Bantam, 1998), to be the single best resource on how to create the space and process for conversations that move to the deepest levels and develop a strong sense of community. She describes the circle this way: "A circle is not just a meeting with the chairs rearranged.... A circle is a way of doing things differently than we have become accustomed to. It is a return to our original form of community. In circle, we rediscover an ancient process of consultation and communion that, for tens of thousands of years, has held the human community together and shaped its course." I encourage you to read her book and visit her website at www.peerspirit.com

Juanita Brown, with her partner David Isaacs and many others around the world, has pioneered the process of "The World Café." Many years ago, Juanita worked with Cesar Chavez and the United Farmworkers to support migrant farm workers in claiming their rights for fair wages and safe working conditions. She has applied her community organizing experience as a learning partner with senior leaders in corporate, academic, and government settings. Early on, Juanita came to understand that large change efforts begin at kitchen tables and informal conversations about the issues that people care about. Juanita explains that we need to focus on "conversations that matter and questions that travel well." The World Café is a process for creating change that is rooted in living systems theory and the human need for conversation. Small, intimate conversations are hosted among large groups of people. As these small café conversations are networked together, knowledge grows, a sense of the whole becomes real, and the collective wisdom of the group becomes visible. Please see her articles and website at www.theworldcafe.com

a story from the aztec people of mexico

It is said by our Grandparents that a long time ago there was a great fire in the forests that covered our Earth. People and animals started to run, trying to escape from the fire. Our brother owl, Tecolotl, was running away also when he noticed a small bird hurrying back and forth between the nearest river and the fire. He headed towards this small bird.

He noticed that it was our brother the Quetzal bird, Quetzaltototl, running to the river, picking up small drops of water in his beak, then returning to the fire to throw that tiny bit of water on the flame. Owl approached Quetzal bird and yelled at him: "What are you doing brother? Are you stupid? You are not going to achieve anything by doing this. What are you trying to do? You must run for your life!"

Quetzal bird stopped for a moment and looked at owl, and then answered: "I am doing the best I can with what I have."

It is remembered by our Grandparents that a long time ago the forests that covered our Earth were saved from a great fire by a small Quetzal bird, an owl, and many other animals and people who got together to put out the flames.